Reasons for Listening

David Scarbrough

Cambridge University Press
Cambridge
London   New York   New Rochelle
Melbourne   Sydney

Published by the Press Syndicate of the University of Cambridge
The Pitt Building, Trumpington Street, Cambridge CB2 1RP
32 East 57th Street, New York, NY 10022, USA
10 Stamford Road, Oakleigh, Melbourne 3166, Australia

© Cambridge University Press 1984

First published 1984
Reprinted 1984

Printed in Great Britain
at the University Press, Cambridge

ISBN 0 521 22922 7 Book
ISBN 0 521 22935 9 Set of 2 cassettes

Copyright
The law allows a reader to make a single copy of part of a book for purposes of private study. It does not allow the copying of entire books or the making of multiple copies of extracts. Written permission for any such copying must always be obtained from the publisher in advance.

Acknowledgements

The author and publishers are grateful to the authors, publishers and others who have given permission for the use of copyright material identified in the text. It has not been possible to identify the sources of all the material used and in such cases the publishers would welcome information from copyright owners.

John Bradley and The Federation of British Tape Recordists; BBC Radio Bristol; Clive Chapman for Voices in my Head; David Attenborough for his interview; Michael Parkinson Enterprises for the interview with Michael Parkinson; Michael Avel, Walter Buchanan and Talking Book Services for the Blind for The Mind's Eye; Peter Bastin for Drakesbroughton Hall and The Devil Undone; Alan Duff for The Interview.

For permission to reproduce photographs: BBC Copyright (pages 45 and 51); Barnaby's Picture Library (pages 20 and 27); British Airports Authority (page 6); Bruwel Ltd, 36 Roseneath Rd, London SW11 for the photograph of a mini-brewery (page 25); COI Crown Copyright (page 81); Camera Press photo by Mike Milner (page 16); Department of Agriculture, British Crown Copyright (page 18); Sally and Richard Greenhill (pages 9 and 68); Mansell Collection (page 66); by courtesy of the Royal Association in Aid of the Deaf and Dumb (page 30); Royal National Institute for the Blind (page 58); Homer Sykes (page 79); Syndication International (page 13); Bob Thomas Sports Photography (pages 34 and 76); Topham (pages 37, 41, 47, 60 and 62); Irene Wyndham (page 49).
Cartoons by David Mostyn

SE

Contents

To the student 4

1 Announcements
At the airport 6
At a railway station 9

2 News
News summary 1 13
News summary 2 16
Short summary 1 18
Short summary 2 20

3 Talks
Starting a new life 25
A weekend in London 27
Voices in my head 30

4 Commentaries
Show jumping 34
Football 37
Horse race 41

5 Interviews
David Attenborough 45
Mrs Victor Bruce 47
Renee Wyndham 49
Michael Parkinson 51

6 Telephone messages 1 56

7 Documentaries
The mind's eye 58
May Day 60
A visit to a sausage factory 62

8 Stories
Drakesbroughton Hall 66
The interview 68
The devil undone 70

9 Discussions
Violence in sport 76
Class in Britain and America 79
Sex discrimination 81

10 Telephone messages 2 86

Transcripts 87

Key 126

To the teacher 141
How to use the material 143

To the student

This material is designed to give you realistic practice in your listening skills. It is likely that at some point in the future you will want to or need to listen to the news in English, or listen to announcements at the airport in English, or listen to a documentary or interview in English; the situations included here are therefore realistic for you as a listener.

The recordings are all examples of authentic language that people listen to. The activities that you are asked to carry out after listening represent activities that a listener might reasonably expect to carry out in situations outside the classroom. And the listening practice in each unit provides an effective starting point for all kinds of activities and discussions.

You will see from the contents page that the recordings are grouped in sections which cover most of the main categories of language that people listen to, including discussions, talks and commentaries. There is no need to work systematically through the book; you may select which recordings to work on in each section. If you work on a minimum of one recording from each section you will complete a full course of listening practice.

A wordlist related to each recording follows at the end of each section. This is to help you to understand the recording. But when you hear a word you don't know or aren't sure of, try to guess its meaning before looking it up in the wordlist. The words are listed in the order in which they appear. Note that the meanings given are always those that the word or expression has in that particular context. The emphasis is on overall comprehension and not on a complete understanding of all the details of the language used.

There is a key at the end of the book which provides answers to all the questions.

When you listen to something, in your own or a foreign language, there are usually three stages for you as a listener.

1 There is usually a *reason* for listening. You may want to listen to find out more information about something, for general interest, or for pleasure or entertainment.
2 You listen to the text and try to understand it.

To the student

3 There is then some *result* because you have listened. Perhaps you have learned something or know more about a person or event, or you may feel happy and relaxed because of what you have listened to.

This book and the cassettes can be used equally well in class with a teacher, or by students working on their own. Whether you are working in a group or alone, try to remember the following:

- Always consider the *reason* for listening to each recording. Discuss it with others in your group, or think about it on your own.
- Remember that you don't need to understand every single word of the recording in order to carry out the tasks successfully after listening. General comprehension is the most important thing.

1 ANNOUNCEMENTS

At the airport

Reason for listening

When you travel by air you usually know the time your flight is due to depart, you know the name of the airline you are flying with and you also know your flight number (it is on your ticket). What you do not know is when your flight will be called. You almost always have to sit in the departure lounge and wait. While you are waiting you may have a cup of coffee, read a magazine or talk to friends, but at the same time you are waiting for the announcement of your flight. Your reason for listening is to know when and where to go, or – if your flight is delayed – how long you are going to have to wait.

At the airport

Listening

This is a practical exercise to see how well you can listen and respond to airport announcements. Your teacher will tell you where departure gates 2, 4, 6, 8 and the restaurant are (in different corners of the room). You will choose a flight to go on. You will then wait in the departure lounge and go to a departure gate when you hear your flight called. If you hear that there is a delay in your flight go to the restaurant.
Now follow these instructions:

Part one
1 Choose a number between 1 and 5.
2 Look at page 8 and find the 'ticket' by the number you chose.
3 Make a note of the flight details. This is your flight.
4 Turn back to this page. Now refer only to your note.
5 You are waiting in an English airport departure lounge. Get out a book or a magazine to look at or talk to friends. If you hear your flight called go to the correct gate. If a delay is announced for your flight go to the restaurant, but make a note of how long the delay will be.

Part two
6 Return to your seat and choose a number between 6 and 10. If your flight was not called in part one keep the same ticket and keep waiting. Perhaps your flight will be called during the next part of the exercise.
7 Repeat steps 2–5 above.

Part three
8 Return to your seat and choose a number between 11 and 15. If your flight was not called in part two keep your ticket and keep waiting. Perhaps you will be called during the next part of the exercise.
9 Repeat steps 2–5 above.

After taking three flights you should go on to a different activity. You can return to this exercise at a later date, choosing different numbers to give you more practice.

Announcements

Flight tickets

1. **Air France** AF814
   Paris

2. **Alitalia** A2291
   Milan

3. **Sabena** SN608
   Brussels

4. **British Airways** BA5
   Tokyo

5. **Iberia** IB551
   Madrid

6. **Swissair** SR805
   Zurich

7. **Sabena** SN608
   Brussels

8. **British Airways** BA11
   Singapore

9. **Olympic Airways** OA260
   Athens

10. **Saudia** SV172
    Jeddah

11. **British Airways** BA175
    New York

12. **Austrian Airlines** OS455
    Vienna

13. **Lufthansa** LH067
    Stuttgart

14. **Scandinavian Airlines** SK528
    Stockholm

15. **Olympic Airways** OA260
    Athens

At a railway station

Reason for listening

Loudspeaker announcements at railway stations can be very important. They not only confirm the facts you should already know about the time of your train, its destination and where you have to change, but they also give information about alterations to the expected situation. They tell you about delays and platform alterations for example. When a train comes into the station where you are waiting you cannot always be certain that it is the one you want. The station announcement should tell you.

Announcements

Listening

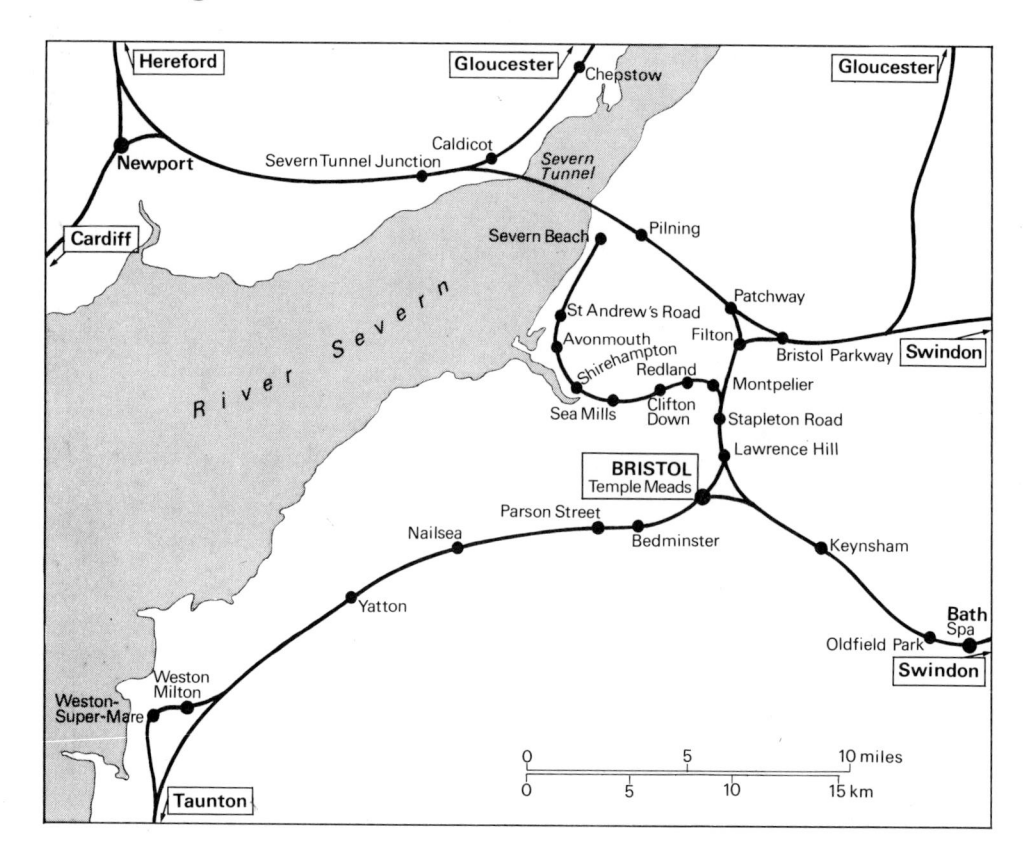

You are at Bristol Temple Meads station and you have the local railway map to help you. Follow these instructions:

Part one
1   Choose a number between 1 and 6.
2   Look at the information opposite and read the section with the number you have chosen.
3   Make a note on a piece of paper of what you need to know.
4   Turn back to this page and now only look at your note and the map.
5   The time is 14.55 and remember, you are at Bristol Temple Meads station. Listen to the first sequence of announcements and when you hear the information you need, write it down.
    Do this now.
6   Check your answer in the Key.

At a railway station

Part two

7 Now choose a number between 7 and 12.
8 Look at the information below and read the section with your number.
9 Make a note as before of the information you need and turn back to this page.
10 The time is now 15.10 and you are again at Bristol Temple Meads station. Listen now to the second sequence of announcements and when you hear the information you need write it down. Do this now.
11 Check your answer in the Key.

Part three

12 Start again at number 1 and choose different numbers.
13 After listening for four different pieces of information leave this exercise and go on to something else.
14 Do the exercise again in about a week's time and listen for four different pieces of information.

Information

1 You are going to Bath Spa. Which platform do you want?
2 You want to go to Pilning. It is on the line to Newport so you expect to be able to get there on the 15.02 to Newport. Are you correct?
3 You are leaving for Gloucester on the 15.02. Where do you have to change?
4 You want to go to Oldfield Park. It is on the line to Bath Spa, so you expect to be able to get there on the 15.15 to Bath Spa. Are you correct?
5 You are waiting on platform 5 for the train to Severn Beach. Is there anything you have to do?
6 When will you be able to leave for Taunton?

7 You are travelling to Gloucester on the 15.29. If you get to the platform just before the train leaves and find all the seats taken will you get on it anyway or wait for the next train? You are not in any hurry.
8 You are going to Severn Beach and you have been told to catch the 15.23. Will you have to change?
9 You are standing on platform 5 waiting for the 15.29 to Gloucester.

Announcements

Someone asks you if they should take this train for Hereford. What is your answer?

10 You are catching the next train to Taunton. How soon can you get on it?

11 You are intending to travel to Cardiff on the 15.20. Will you have to change anywhere?

12 You are in a hurry to get to Bristol Parkway and you are waiting on platform 5 for the 15.29 train. Can you get there any earlier and if so, from which platform?

2 NEWS

News summary 1

Reason for listening

You listen to the news on the radio usually because you have a general interest in knowing what is going on. You may also listen to the news in order to find out what has been happening in a particular place or in relation to a subject that is of special interest to you.

News

Before listening

Choose A, B, C or D before listening to the news.
A You are interested in aeroplanes and are worried about the possibility of accidents when there are so many aeroplanes flying at the same time.
B You are interested in pop music. Your favourite group is called Fantasy.
C You are flying to Fréjus in the South of France tomorrow for a holiday.
D You live in London, in a part called Brixton. You thought you heard police car sirens early this morning.
Now listen to the news. If you hear anything of special interest to you listen carefully so that you can give some information later.

After listening once

If you chose A before listening, answer the questions in section A; if you chose B, answer the questions in section B; and so on. Try to answer all the questions in your section before listening again.

A 1 What aeroplanes were nearly involved in an accident recently?
   2 Where did the incident take place?
   3 Whose fault was it?
   4 Where did the passenger plane take off from?
   5 How many aeroplanes were involved?
   6 How close did the aeroplanes get?

B 1 Where did this incident take place?
   2 What were the people outside waiting for?
   3 How were people injured?
   4 Was anybody killed?
   5 Why did the concert continue as planned?
   6 Why are the organisers of the concert being criticised?
   7 Are Fantasy going to continue their tour of the U.S.?

C 1 What is happening between Fréjus and Cannes?
   2 How many people have been involved?
   3 Who is now going to help them?
   4 You were going to stay at a holiday home in the hills, leaving tomorrow. Do you think you should go?
   5 Will it all be over by the time you arrive?

News summary 1

D 1 Who are the police chasing?
 2 What had they done?
 3 How was a policeman injured?
 4 What did the robbers use to escape in?
 5 How much money did they escape with?
 6 What did the robbers do with their car?

Other news items
When you have answered the questions in your section see how many of the following questions you can answer about other news items.
1 What was there to interest football fans in the news today?
2 Why would supporters of Liverpool football team be interested in the news?
3 Motorists in the centre of London had a slow journey for a while this morning. What was it that possibly delayed them?
4 How many people were in Trafalgar Square this morning?
5 This is a banner carried by one of the people in Trafalgar Square. What are the missing words?

```
  ----------
    AGAINST
  ----------
```

6 Someone has just offered a jeweller in London a diamond, an emerald and two rubies at a very low price. The jeweller is now phoning Scotland Yard. Why?

News summary 2

Reason for listening

You listen to the news on the radio usually because you have a general interest in knowing what is going on. You may also listen to the news in order to find out what has been happening in a particular place or in relation to a subject that is of special interest to you.

Before listening

Choose A, B, C or D before listening the first time.
A You are a television engineer and you have been on strike for some time.
B A friend of yours drives a security van. You often tell him his job is dangerous and that he ought to change it.
C You are making a special study of the violent behaviour of football supporters.
D You are flying to Italy tomorrow for a holiday near Florence.
Now listen to the news. If you hear anything of special interest to you listen carefully so that you can give some information later.

News summary 2

After listening once

If you chose A before listening, answer the questions in section A. If you chose B answer the questions in that section and so on. Try to answer all the questions in your section before listening again.

A 1 Do you work for the BBC or Independent Television?
   2 When and where are the talks starting?
   3 Who is presenting new proposals at the talks?
   4 Is the General Secretary of your union expecting the talks to succeed?

B 1 Why was the security van in a narrow street off Piccadilly?
   2 How did the thieves stop the security van?
   3 Were the thieves armed?
   4 How much money did they steal?
   5 What condition were the driver of the van and his assistant in afterwards?

C 1 Did the reported violence take place during a match?
   2 Had the supporters' teams been playing each other?
   3 What started the trouble?
   4 How was the fighting stopped?
   5 What is one possible result of this incident for Manchester supporters?

D 1 Has any damage been caused by the earthquake in Florence?
   2 When did the earthquake take place?
   3 Why have a lot of places been cut off as a result of the earthquake?
   4 Has anybody been killed?
   5 Were any buildings destroyed or made unusable?

Other news items

When you have answered the questions in your section, see how many of the following questions you can answer about other items.

1 a) When and where did a DC10 airliner crash?
  b) Was anybody still alive after the crash?
  c) What caused the accident?
2 a) When will the next General Election take place?
  b) Why was this announcement made last night?
3 a) People are voting for a Member of Parliament in London South-West today. In which Parliament will the successful candidate sit?
  b) Why was this by-election necessary?
  c) Did the previous member win his election easily?

News

Short summary 1

Reason for listening

Some radio stations give very short news summaries between programmes. For example, BBC Radio 1 broadcasts popular music most of the day and its news summaries contain mostly general interest items rather than serious political news.

Short summary 1

After listening

Complete the following conversation about the news with another member of your group. For example:

A: Did you hear about hospital waiting lists?

B: Yes, ...
         (they've gone up by a quarter in the last five years.)

Take part A or B. When you have finished, repeat the conversation with another member of your group. Change parts this time.
If you are working alone, speak the words aloud when you practise giving the answers.

1 A: Did you hear about the demonstration in Corby?

   B: Yes, ...

2 A: Are the unions doing anything about it?

   B: Well, they're ....

3 A: I see the EEC is giving Britain some money.

   B: Yes, ...

4 A: It's all going to England, isn't it?

   B: ....

5 A: Isn't it amazing that people are still bringing animals into the country illegally?

   B: ....

News

Short summary 2

Reason for listening

Some radio stations give very short news summaries between programmes. For example, BBC Radio 1 broadcasts popular music most of the day and its news summaries contain mostly general interest items rather than serious political news.

Short summary 2

After listening

Complete the following conversation about the news with another member of your group. Take part A or B.
When you have finished, repeat the conversation with another member of your group. Change parts this time.
If you are working alone, speak the words aloud when you practise giving the answers.

1. A: I hear the owner of that stately home near Stevenage got into trouble over a pop concert.

   B: Yes, he ……………………………………………………………………

2. A: Transplant operations seem to be getting more and more common, don't they?

   B: Yes, ……………………………………………………………………

3. A: Did you hear about the storms up north last night?

   B: Yes, ……………………………………………………………………

4. A: Well, let's hope the bad weather is over now.

   B: Well, ……………………………………………………………………

5. A: It's getting really dangerous to be a teacher these days. Did you hear what happened in Surrey this morning?

   B: Yes, ……………………………………………………………………

6. A: It's lucky she didn't actually fire the gun.

   B: Well, ……………………………………………………………………

Wordlist

News summary 1

constable   an ordinary policeman
shattered   broken into many pieces
pursuing   following and trying to catch
raided   attacked, robbed
branch   large banks have branches in every town; an office
made their getaway   escaped
fans   people with a strong interest; enthusiasts
went ahead   continued as planned
spokesman   someone who speaks in public for a person or group
calling off   deciding not to do something that was planned
formation   a group
colliding   running into each other; crashing
scheduled flight   a normal airline flight that takes place at the same time at regular intervals
cockpit   the part of the plane where the pilot sits
claimed the life of   killed
rage   burn strongly (a fire)
fanned (by winds)   the winds are making the fire burn more strongly
blaze   strong fire
race prejudice   dislike of people of a different nationality, usually also with different physical features (e.g. colour of skin)
drew   attracted, brought together
ethnic groups   people from the same racial and cultural group
mailbag   a bag that letters and parcels are carried in
went missing   got lost
dealer   a person who buys and sells a product
draw   (in sport) when it is decided which teams will play against each other in a competition

News summary 2

speculation   guessing, using the imagination
avalanches   falls of snow or earth and rocks
cables   thick wires that carry electricity
ambushed   was stopped and then attacked unexpectedly

Wordlist

rammed   was driven into
short cut   a quick way
flight recorder   the instrument that keeps details of an aeroplane's flight
impact   the moment when the plane hit the ground
by-election   an election to replace one Member of Parliament
majority   the difference in the number of votes for the winner and for the person who came second in the election
formula   way; method
get under way   start
negotiations   discussions
eye witnesses   people who saw what happened
rival   in competition with each other
insult   call each other names and generally be rude to
broken out   begun
boarded   got on
withdrawing   taking out of service
soccer specials   trains specially arranged for supporters going to football matches

Short summary 1

Northamptonshire   a county in the middle of England
steel works   steel factory; place where they make steel
closure plans   plans to close the factory
hospital waiting lists   lists of people waiting to go into hospital
EEC   European Economic Community; often called the Common Market
rabies   a disease that causes madness in dogs and other animals and can be passed on to people
hamster   a small furry animal kept as a pet
derailed   which has come off the rails
disrupted   broken (the service)

Short summary 2

shotgun   a sporting gun that shoots a lot of small balls of lead
Surrey   a county south of London
double-barrelled   the barrel of a gun is the metal tube that the bullet comes out of – this gun had two barrels
threatened   said she was going to shoot them

News

overpowered   she was brought under control by the police who were too strong for her
surgeons   doctors who do operations
transplant   take a part out of one body and put it in another
organ   a part of the body that has an important purpose; other organs are the heart and lungs
diabetes   a disease of the pancreas (an organ) in which there is more sugar in the blood than can be used
liver   another organ; this one cleans the blood
kidney   the organ that removes waste liquid from the blood
stately home   a large house in the country built some time ago; often visited by the public
fined   was made to pay some money
magistrates   people who act as judges in the lowest courts
£25 costs   because he lost his case he had to pay the costs of the police who spoke against him; so he had to pay an extra £25
sweeping across   moving quickly
collapsed   fell down
are forecast   are expected

3   TALKS

Starting a new life

Reason for listening

Listening to another person talking about his experiences can be useful to us in our own lives. Nigel Fitz-Hugh left a safe job in London, moved to a small village in South Devon and started an unusual but very successful one-man business.

Talks

After listening

1 Discuss these questions in your group and try to agree on the answers.
   a) When Nigel Fitz-Hugh moved to Devon how did he feel about the job he used to do?
   b) How did he come to choose making dog beds as his first venture?
   c) Why did he stop making dog beds?
   d) What made him choose brewing beer as his next venture?
   e) Is he likely to give up brewing for something else?
   f) Why does he do all the work himself?

2 What are the reasons for Nigel Fitz-Hugh's success? Discuss this question with other students and make some notes as you go along.

3 A friend of yours wants to give up a safe job and set up in business alone making and selling computer games. Discuss with your group what advice you can give. Use what you have heard Nigel Fitz-Hugh say. Write to your friend saying what you think about the idea.

A weekend in London

Reason for listening

You have booked a weekend holiday in London and the tour organisers have sent you a recorded description of the programme together with a map.

Listening

Listen to the information and use the map to help you see where you are going to be and what you will be able to do.
The tour company has forgotten to send you the written summary of the weekend arrangements mentioned at the end of the recording, so your

Talks

main task now is to write one out for yourself. Put down the main events on the plan below. Remember to include the times when the guide will be starting the visits.

	MORNING	AFTERNOON	EVENING
FRIDAY			
SATURDAY			
SUNDAY			

After listening

1 The plan shows what it is possible for you to do during your weekend. You have to decide, however, what *you* want to do. You don't have to go with the guide all the time and you have a choice of things to do on some occasions.
So make another plan set out like the one above that shows how *you* have decided to organise your weekend. Make sure you include starting times and meeting places if you decide to go with the tour guide. Mark on the map as many of the places you are going to visit as you can find. Write down underneath your plan the two pieces of advice the guide gave you on the cassette.

2 Compare your programme with other students and discuss the reasons for your choices.

A weekend in London

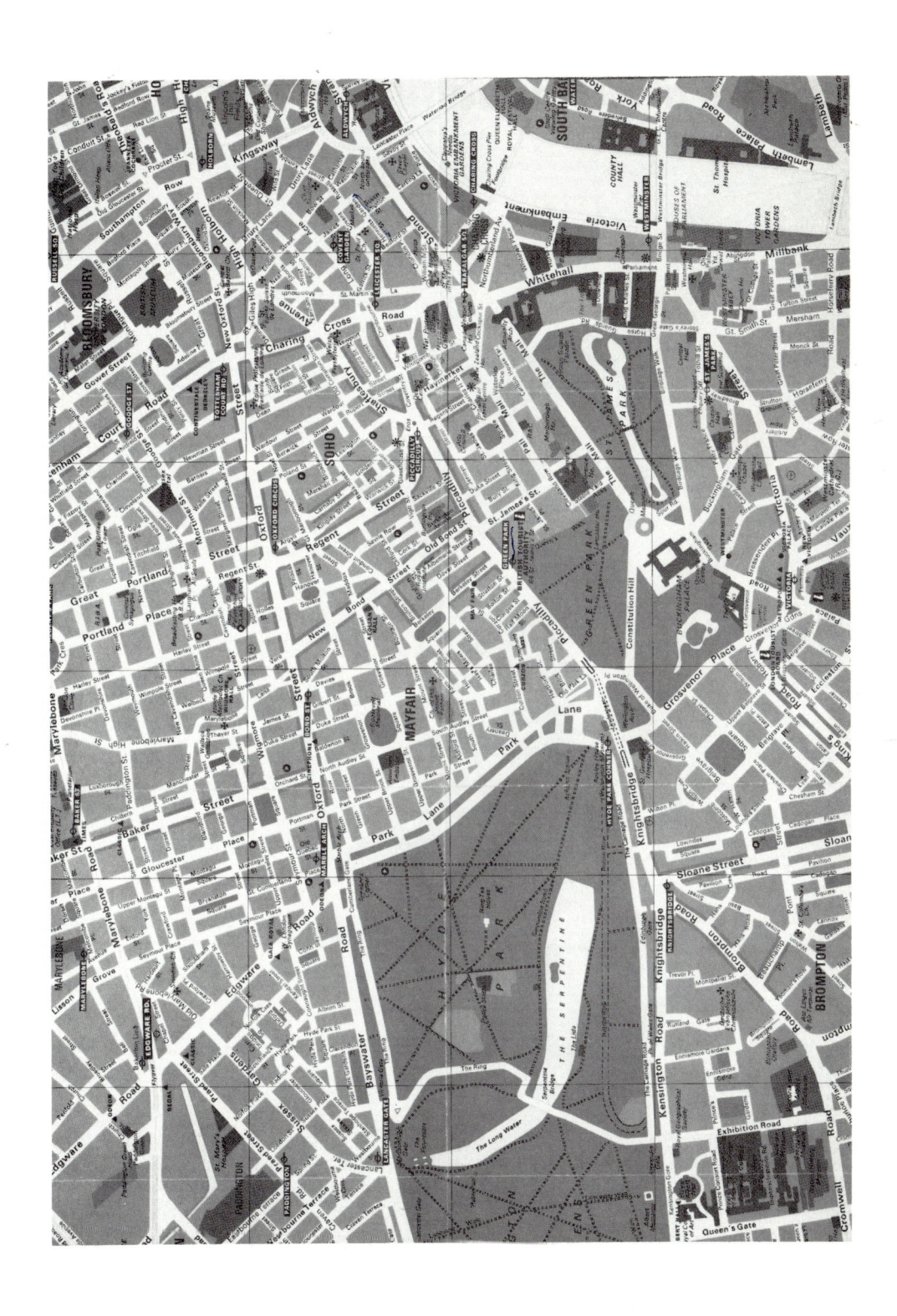

Talks

Voices in my head

Reason for listening

The reason for listening to this talk may be that you are interested in one man's story about himself. You may also be interested to know what it is like to be deaf.

Voices in my head

After listening

1 If you have followed the main points of Mr X's story, you should be able to answer these questions.
   a) How bad was his deafness?
   b) What caused his deafness?
   c) Where was he being treated?
   d) What did he finally do which led to the recovery of his hearing?

2 Discuss the following statements in your group, using the speaker's experience to provide ideas and examples. If you are working alone write down a few brief points for each statement.
   a) The trouble with being deaf is that people cannot *see* that there is anything wrong with you.
   b) When you cannot understand what people are saying they think you are stupid.
   c) It is easy to think that people are laughing at you when you are deaf.
   d) People could make things easier for deaf or partially deaf people if they tried.
   e) You can soon begin to feel very lonely when you go deaf.
   f) There is more to understanding people than just hearing the words.
   g) It is not always easy to get a second opinion on your condition although it is usually worth it.

Wordlist

Starting a new life

sag bag   a bag filled with beans for sitting on
mail order   sell things through the post
itchy feet   a desire to something different
brewery   a place where beer is made (brewed)
a head start   an advantage over other people
it went off like a bomb   it was very successful
flattering   they really have a high opinion of him
venture   business activity; a project

A weekend in London

freshen up   have a wash and make yourself feel fresh again
at 7.30 sharp   at exactly 7.30
strolling   walking slowly in a relaxed way
traffic intersection   where several roads cross
straight play   a serious piece of writing for the theatre (not a musical)
tin whistle   a cheap flute made of metal
tiara   a little crown of jewels sometimes worn by women in their hair

Voices in my head

partial   not complete
abscess   a bubble in the skin full of unpleasant liquid caused by disease or injury
scab   the covering of dried blood that forms where the skin has been broken
restricted   it was not as good as it used to be
eardrum   the piece of skin in the ear that receives sounds
recede   move to the background; be reduced
law of the jungle   the law that says the strongest wins
despising   hating a person you consider inferior
articulate   pronounce words clearly
at the best of times   when they are doing it as well as they can
wadding up   making the pieces into balls
couldn't stand   hated

Wordlist

isolated   cut off; left alone
(used the) pose (of)   put an expression on his face that wasn't real
vacant/abstracted   with your thoughts in another place
withdrew from   took less and less part in
out-patient   someone who goes to hospital to see a doctor and then goes home again
treating   was looking after him
recommendation from someone personally   when someone you know tells you someone or something is good
second opinion   opinion of another doctor, to see if he agreed with the first doctor
a fiver   a £5 note
drastic   remarkable; unexpected; terrible
showed up   became known
the improvement ... was marked   a very clear and definite improvement
did wonders for   had a very good effect on
self-confidence   belief in himself
tone (of voice)   the sound of a voice that tells you something about the speaker – is he angry, happy, sad?
texture (of voice)   the quality of a voice – is it harsh, soft, pure?
grunts   the noise you might make, for example, if you have to make a great effort to lift something
subtlety   all the extra information you get from hearing how a person speaks in addition to the straight meaning of the words
mumble and mutter and swallow their words   words used to describe the noises people make when they do not speak clearly because they do not open their mouths enough

4 COMMENTARIES

Show jumping

Reason for listening

You will listen to this commentary if you have an interest in show jumping and you want to know how each horse and rider performs.

Listening

1 Listen to both parts of the commentary then answer these questions.
   a) Which horse was more successful?
   b) How far did the second horse get before knocking any fences down?
   c) What was the weather like?
   d) How many faults did each rider get?

Show jumping

2 Listen to the commentary on the second rider again. What does the commentator tell us about him?
   a) How old is he?
   b) Is this his only horse in the competition?
   c) What sort of jump do we know the horse Dartmoor is particularly good at?

After listening

1 Mark on the diagram the fences that each horse hit. Were any fences knocked down by both horses? Does this mean that some were more difficult than others? Discuss the fences with the others in your group then write a few sentences about the course that they had to jump.

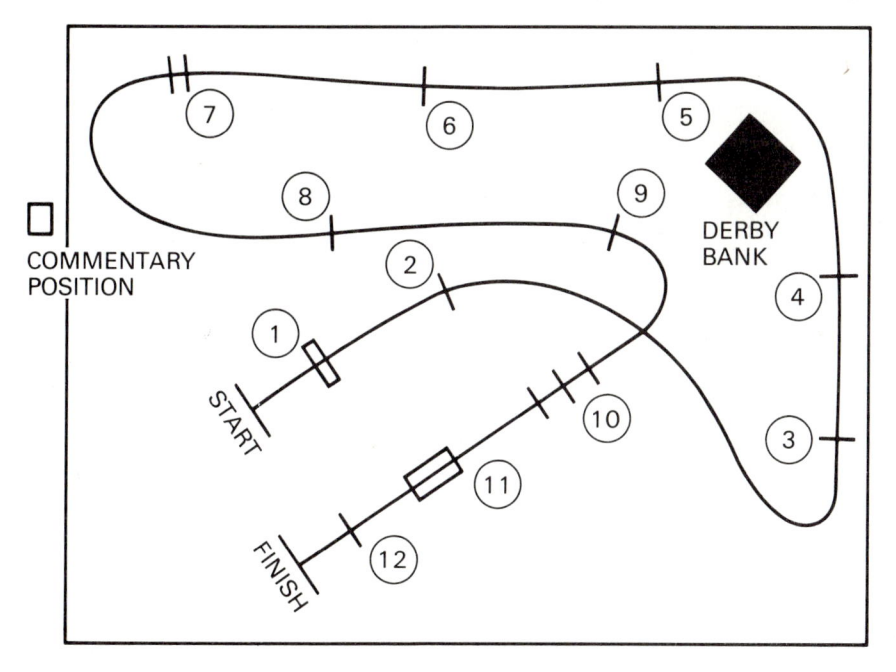

2 If you are particularly interested in show jumping here is an exercise about some of the fences the horses had to jump.
Look at the pictures of some typical show jumping fences. They illustrate the type of fences used for numbers 1, 2/5, 3, 6, 8, 9/12 and 11 in the competition you have listened to. Match the type of fence with the right number.

35

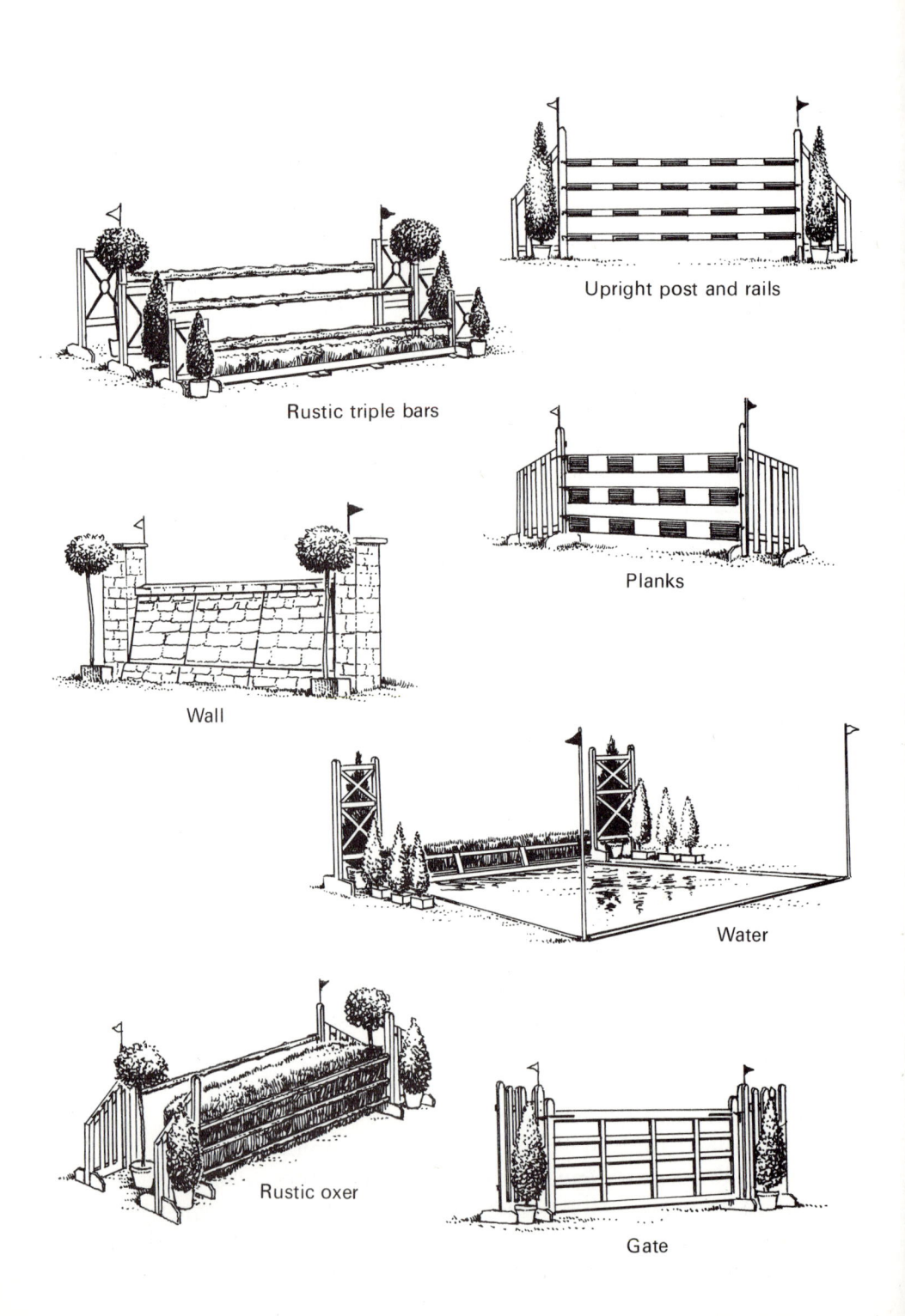

Commentaries

Upright post and rails

Rustic triple bars

Planks

Wall

Water

Rustic oxer

Gate

Football

Reason for listening

You normally listen to a football match because you are generally interested in football and you want to know the result of the match. You probably want to be able to talk about the game afterwards, so you want to know how well the players performed, who scored, who helped score, who nearly scored, who prevented a score and what will happen next.

Listening

1 Listen to the extracts from a commentary on a semi-final match in the Football Association Cup Competition. The two teams are Liverpool and Manchester United. The commentary begins in the second half of the match. Choose the team that you would like to win.

37

Commentaries

Listen to all three extracts then answer these general questions.
a) What was the final score?
b) Which team scored the last goal of the match?
c) When did Manchester United score their second goal?
d) Who scored Manchester United's second goal?
e) Who scored Liverpool's second goal?
f) In which half of the field was most of the match played after Manchester United scored their second goal?

After listening once

1 Listen to the recording again and write down the name of the team that each of the following footballers plays for.

Alan Hansen	Steve Coppel	Arthur Albiston
Gordon McQueen	Jimmy Greenhof	Kenny Dalglish
Gary Bailey	Brian Greenhof	Terry McDermott
Phil Neal	Emlyn Hughes	
Ray Kennedy	Steve Heighway	

2 Listen to each section of the commentary again and correct the following statements if necessary.

First section
a) Liverpool have been in four Cup Finals in eight years.
b) Manchester United have been in two Cup Finals in four years.
c) Liverpool beat United in the Cup Final two years ago.
d) Arthur Albiston replaced Houston in the Cup Final two years ago.
e) Jimmy Greenhof scored for Manchester United.
f) Manchester United are an experienced side.
g) The Liverpool side is not so experienced.
h) Bob Paisley is Liverpool's manager.

Second section
a) With eight minutes to go the score was 5–3.
b) Alan Hansen comes from Wales.
c) He used to play for a team called Partick Thistle.
d) Alan Hansen has scored a lot of goals this season.
e) Liverpool scored seven minutes from the end of the match.

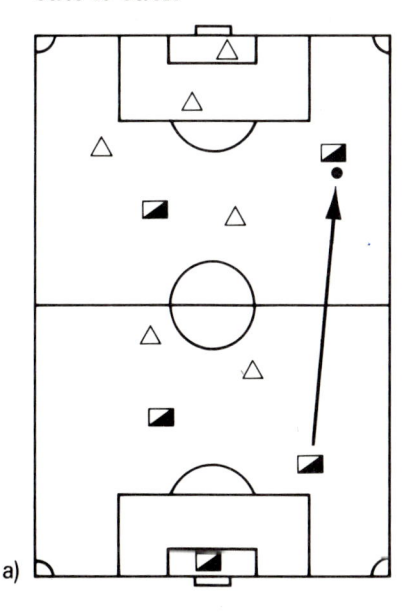

Football

Third section
a) The match finished at the end of 90 minutes.
b) Manchester United got a free kick when Hughes brought down one of their players.
c) Liverpool are a team that cannot stand pressure.
d) This was the last match of the season between Liverpool and Manchester United.

3 This question is only for people who are interested in the special vocabulary of football.

In the following diagrams ◤ represents a Liverpool player;
△ represents a Manchester United player;
• represents the ball.

Each diagram illustrates one of the expressions used in the commentary for movement of the ball. Which diagram illustrates which football expression?

a long ball down field   gone out of play
lays it square   a corner
lobs it   a loose ball
hits it home   a goal kick
cuts it back

39

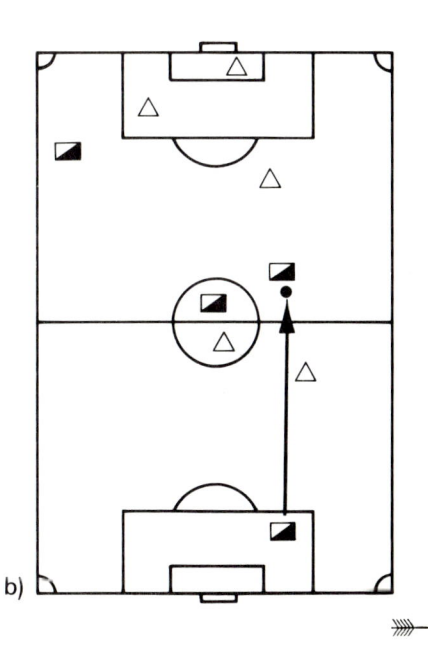

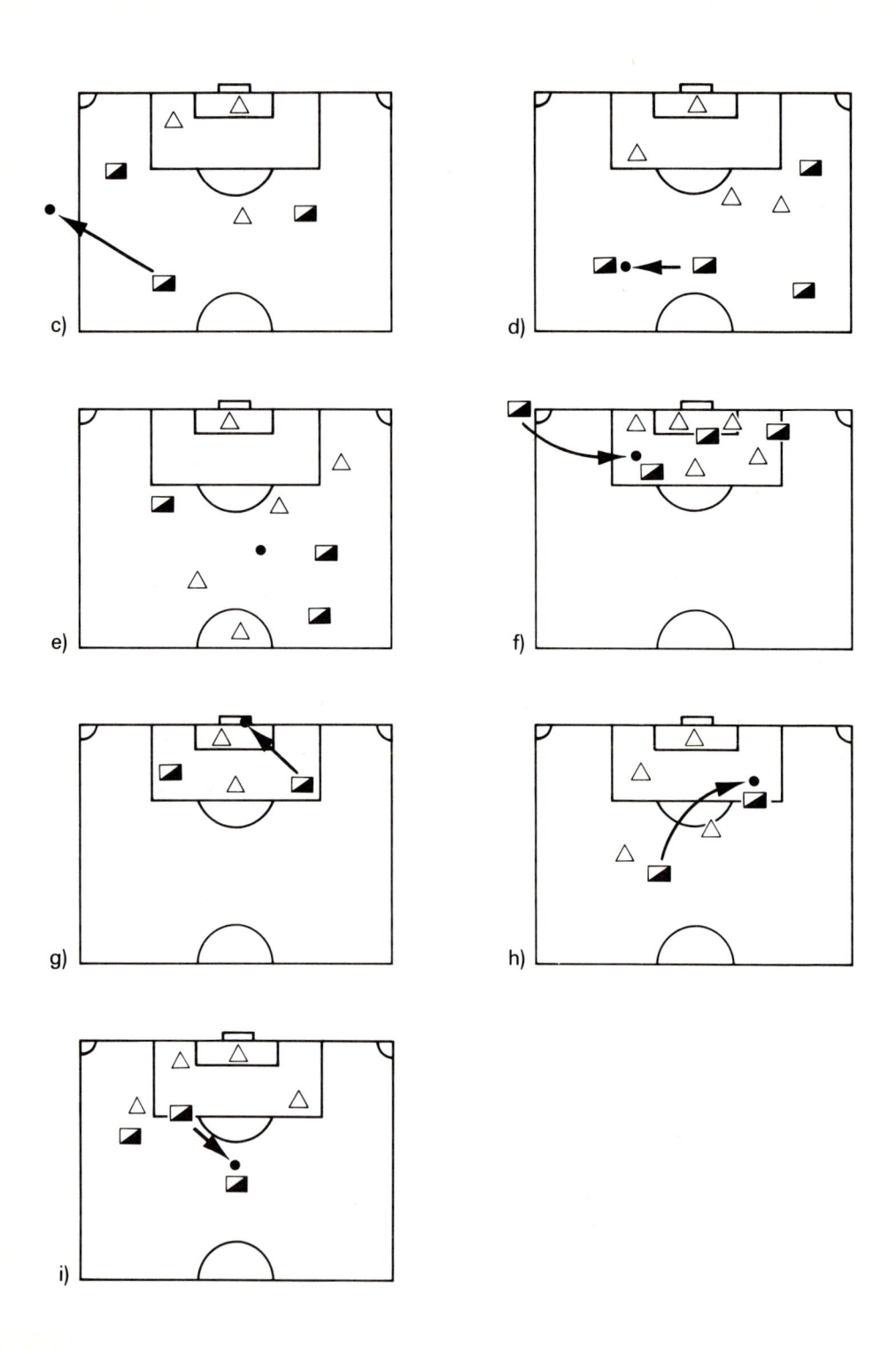

Commentaries

c)

d)

e)

f)

g)

h)

i)

Horse race

Reason for listening

You will listen to this commentary if you have an interest in horse racing and you want to know how each horse performs.

Commentaries

Before listening

Work in groups. Each member of the group should choose one of the horses in the race from the list below. Your main interest as you listen to the commentary is to find out what position your horse finishes in.

List of runners
Effulgence
Fluellin
Jellaby
Palimon
Rhyme Royal
Swiss Maid
Sexton Blake

After listening once

1 Check where the horses chosen by the members of your group finished. Make a list of the final position of *all* the horses in the race.

2 A number of expressions used in describing the race are used in many other situations. Listen to the commentary again and notice when each of the following expressions is used. Then suggest another situation outside horse racing when all the expressions might be used. Have a discussion in your group using this new situation and make sure you include all the expressions.

under starter's orders
make the early running
set a terrific pace
take them on
bring up the rear
make no headway

Wordlist

Show jumping

stood right back   the horse was a long way from the fence when it began to jump
ploughs through   goes through the fence instead of over it
faults   penalty points
ditch   a long, narrow hole usually with water in it
rustic natural poles   natural branches of trees
sails over   jumps over without difficulty
planks   long, thin pieces of wood
a good foot to spare   the horse jumped at least a foot higher than necessary
clear   'a clear round'; a round with no penalty points
Olympia   a stadium in London where important show jumping competitions are held
the Puissance   a competition with particularly high fences
packed out   full of people
open stand   a place for spectators to sit, but without a roof
divots   pieces of grass and earth dug up by the horses as they jump

Football

bidding   attempting, trying
F.A.   Football Association
prods it   kicks it in a controlled way, moving the ball a fairly short distance
clumsy   not very graceful; no one was very sure what was going to happen
the box   the penalty area in front of the goal marked with white lines
come of age   grow up; become mature
jinx   something which brings bad luck; Liverpool have found it difficult to beat Manchester United in the past
the touchline   the line down the side of the pitch
play his ace   in most card games the ace is the most valuable card; Bob Paisley is the manager of Liverpool and is going to bring on a very good player in order to try to win
tackled   an attempt to take the ball away from an opposing player

43

Commentaries

cup-tie a match in a competition for a cup
injury-time time added on to a match to make up for time lost dealing with injured players
checks his stride slows down
on-side a player is on-side if he has the goal keeper and at least one other player between him and the opposing goal when he receives the ball
cannons off the ball hits someone or something and bounces back
deadlock neither side has the advantage; they have failed to achieve a result

Horse race

break when they leave the starting position
stalls starting machine divided into boxes for the horses so that they all start from the same position
back straight the straight part of the race course opposite the finishing point
rousted along forced to go faster
stand rails on the side of the track closest to the stand (which is where the spectators sit)
furlong one-eighth of a mile
comes storming through comes through very quickly
going to tell going to be important

5 INTERVIEWS

David Attenborough

Reason for listening

The reason for listening to this interview is to find out what an interesting person like David Attenborough thinks about the subject of change in a person's life. David Attenborough is a very popular writer and film-maker on television in Britain. He specialises in Natural History.

Interviews

After listening

1 Discuss the following points in your group.
   a) David Attenborough describes two kinds of change that people meet in their lives. Say briefly what they are.
   b) What are the three parts of the world that he is particularly fond of? Which would *you* most like to visit and why?
   c) What does David Attenborough think are the 'happiest times'?
   d) What happens when things do not change anymore?
   e) Can you avoid change?
   f) Why do you think David Attenborough accepted a job in the management of TV?
   g) What are some of the ways people might be changed 'willy-nilly'?
   h) What are some of the targets people can set themselves?

2 What do you think David Attenborough would say in response to the following opinions?
   a) The best thing to do is find the place in the world you like best and stay there.
   b) Happiness is a life without change.
   c) 'I make films for TV. You won't get me into a desk job'.
   d) There is no way you can change your life.
   e) You can avoid change in your life if you are very careful.

Mrs Victor Bruce

Reason for listening

The reason for listening to this interview is to find out what one remarkable old lady thought about the struggle by women in Britain just before the First World War to be given the right to vote in elections.

Interviews

After listening

1 In groups, discuss these questions and try to agree on the answers.
   a) What did Mrs Bruce think men and women should be concerned with?
   b) What was her reaction to seeing suffragettes chained to the railings in Downing Street?
   c) How did she feel if people called her a suffragette?
   d) What did people do when the suffragettes marched?
   e) In what sort of activity did Mrs Bruce like to compete with men?

2 How many things does this interview tell us about suffragettes? (5 or 6 points)

3 How much does this interview tell us about Mrs Bruce's life and opinions? Make two lists:
   a) Mrs Bruce's life;
   b) Her opinions.

4 Which view of Mrs Bruce does your group take – if either?
   a) A woman of strong character like Mrs Bruce should have given her support to the suffragette movement.
   b) Mrs Bruce was quite right not to join the suffragette movement. She was too much of an individualist.

Renee Wyndham

Reason for listening

The reason for listening to this interview is to find out what Renee Wyndham has to say about travel and then perhaps compare it with your own experience. Renee Wyndham is a journalist, singer and song-writer who works as a radio and television news and current affairs presenter.

Interviews

After listening

Discuss these questions in your group and try to agree on the answers.
1 After saying how many countries she has visited and mentioning two places she would like to go back to, the rest of the interview can be divided into three main sections each dealing with a different topic. What are these three topics?
2 What are some of the ways the cost of travelling can be reduced?
3 Have you ever been to any of the places that Renee Wyndham mentions? Tell the rest of the group about your experiences there.
4 Which of the two places Renee Wyndham would like to re-visit would you most like to go to and why?
5 Where in the world would you most like to go to and how would you prefer to travel there?
6 Which of Renee Wyndham's dangerous experiences seemed most frightening to you and why?
7 Tell the group about any dangerous experiences you have had while travelling.
8 Renee Wyndham says you learn a lot about yourself when you travel and this is because of the things you are free from. What sort of things are you free from when you travel?

Michael Parkinson

Reason for listening

The reason for listening to this interview is to find out what Michael Parkinson can tell us about running a successful talk-show on television. He is a well-known television personality. For many years he has had a regular programme on BBC television in which he interviews famous people, including filmstars, writers and sports personalities. This sort of programme is called a 'talk-show' or, sometimes, a 'chat-show'.

Interviews

Listening

First make a list of the five questions that the interviewer asks Michael Parkinson.

After listening

1 When you have the five questions, you also have the five aspects of running a talk-show on television that Michael Parkinson talks about. Can you now write down the main points he makes, leaving out specific examples and details?
 The first one is done for you:

   Q. 1 An interviewer must have curiosity. It helps to have a journalist's training and another important thing is to be able to get on with people.

2 Now a few questions about some of the other things Michael Parkinson said. You should not have included these in the main points you wrote down in question 1.
   a) Does he give the impression that a lot of people have been successful at running talk-shows or that many people have failed?
   b) What would you make a fortune from if you could put it into bottles?
   c) Why was it difficult interviewing Robert Mitchum and how did Michael Parkinson manage to get through the interview?

Wordlist

David Attenborough

wear off   get less and less: you may take an aspirin if you have a headache; after a while the effect of the aspirin *wears off* and you may begin to feel the headache again
limitation   fault; something that is wrong with human beings
have the option   ability to choose
frustrated   feeling annoyed and irritated because you cannot do something you want to do
creative artist   a person like a painter or a writer who produces something new and artistic
corny phrase   an overused expression; a cliché
nonetheless   nevertheless; in any case
care about   have a deep interest in
network   TV channel
quid   popular slang for £, a pound; £20 is 'twenty quid'
can't help being   there is nothing they can do about it
bogged down   stuck
willy-nilly   whether you like it or not; there is nothing you can do about it
set yourself targets   decide on something you want to do or achieve in the future

Mrs Victor Bruce

suffragette   popular word for a woman who joined the fight for the vote
militant   active; prepared to demonstrate, violently if necessary
governess   a woman working as a private teacher in a family
Downing Street   the Prime Minister of Britain has his/her official residence at number 10 Downing Street
railings   a metal fence
in the long term   finally; in the end
vocations   careers; occupations
boos   if you should 'Boo!' at someone (with a long *oo*) it shows that you do not like them or you disapprove of them
clapping   making a noise with your hands to show you approve of someone and of what they do
the exclusive preserve of the man   something that only men are expected to do

Interviews

Brooklands   a former motor racing track of the 1920s and 30s
Sir Henry Seagrave, Frazer Nash   famous British racing drivers and car designers

Renee Wyndham

hitchhike   travel by asking people in cars and lorries to take you with them
loads of   plenty; a large amount
feel like   had a desire to do something; wanted to
unspoilt   countryside that has remained in a natural state
bounds of routine   your regular timetable
assumptions   what people expect you to be or do
inhibitions   thoughts and feelings that stop you doing things
taste   what a person likes doing; or what a person likes
loo   popular word for lavatory, toilet
stabbed   someone had stuck a knife in him
voluntarily   she did it because she wanted to; nobody forced her to do it
the Middle East war   a war between Israel and the Arab States
living on a knife edge   in a very dangerous situation
contemplating coolly   calmly considering
air raid   an attack from the air with bombs
gadding around   travelling from place to place and enjoying it
put me up   let me stay with them; give me a bed
reciprocate   do the same for them
rough it   live in an uncomfortable way
sleep out   sleep in the open, in a field or park perhaps
entertain the natives   sing for the local people
proceeds   the money you get from some activity
Radio 3   one of the BBC radio channels
(the money comes) rolling in   the money arrives; it gives the feeling that quite a lot of money comes in without having to do much for it

Michael Parkinson

prerequisite   something you need before you start
curiosity   wanting to know everything about someone or something
not assumed   genuine; not artificial
graveyard   place where people are buried

littered with them   full of them; they are 'all over the place'
tombstones   stones marking graves
argues that   means
comes into play   must be considered
affinity with   a friendly and sympathetic relationship with
on air   while the show is in progress
watch it back   see the recording
right shot   right picture
research   preparation; finding out about the person to be interviewed
wing it   make it up as you go along (TV slang)
aide memoire   a set of notes
block out   write down some general points
the aforesaid   who I talked about before
spin off   move off unexpectedly
on point duty   directing traffic
I envy them   I wish I was one of them
talent   special ability
ambition   desire to do something in the future (usually something that will make you famous)

6   TELEPHONE MESSAGES 1

Reason for listening

Unlike most of the material in this book these are not messages that you intend or expect to listen to. You usually receive telephone messages unexpectedly. They come suddenly and quickly and you have to listen to and make a note of the information contained in the message – particularly when the message is for someone else.

Note

There are twelve telephone messages in all. Six are grouped together at the end of each cassette. Use them as extra practice between the main units of the course.

Telephone messages

Before listening

The phone messages are not for you. They are for someone called Horatio Hamilton. Horatio is living in the same house as you in England, but he is often out while you are often in. When you answer the telephone in this house the caller often wants Horatio. The caller always seems to be in a hurry and has no time to repeat the message.
Your job is to make a note of the information as accurately as you can so that you can pass it on to Horatio later.

For each message you should imagine that you have just answered the phone and the conversation has gone like this:

You: Hello?
Caller: Can I speak to Horatio (or Mr Hamilton) please?
You: I'm afraid he's out at the moment.
Caller: .... (as on the recording) ....

Listening

Listen to the telephone message ONCE and then immediately write down the message for Horatio.

After listening

1 Exchange your version of the message with someone else and see if there are any differences.
2 Put all the messages in your group together and agree on exactly what the message was.
3 Listen to the recording again. If you want to check that you have the correct information you can look at the transcript of the message on page 110.

If you are working alone.
1 Write the message down after hearing it once.
2 If you are not sure you have the right information listen to the recording again.
3 Check with the transcript on page 110.

7 DOCUMENTARIES

The mind's eye

Reason for listening

After listening to this documentary you should expect to know how the Talking Books for the Blind scheme works as well as understanding some of the technical details about the equipment that is used.

The mind's eye

After listening

1 You should now be able to persuade a blind friend to join the Talking Book scheme. So answer your friend's questions and worries. Practise with a partner first, then write down your conversation.

'I don't suppose they've got any books that would interest me.'

'What sort of people make the recordings?'

'But I'm going to study economics. They can't help me with that, can they?'

'I'm hopeless with machines. I'm sure it would be much too complicated.'

'But what happens if something goes wrong?'

2 Now give your blind friend a complete description of the Talking Book machine and the cassettes that go with it.

N.B. The Talking Book Service has introduced new technical equipment since this recording was made.

Documentaries

May Day

Reason for listening

The reason for listening to this documentary is to find out what happens in one part of Britain on May 1st. You will learn something about a traditional form of dancing called Morris dancing.

After listening

1 Name three places where you would be able to watch the Morris dancers in Shoreham on May Day morning.

May Day

2 The following information about Morris dancing was written by someone who knew very little about it. You should now be able to rewrite this account correcting all the mistakes.

> Morris dancing existed all over England, Scotland and Wales and became most popular during the nineteenth century. There is a long tradition of Morris dancing in Sussex, but in the Cotswolds it is called 'step dancing'.
> The dancers used to black their faces and people had to try to guess who they were. It seems fairly certain that because of their black faces they were called 'Moorish' dancers and this word later changed to 'Morris'.
> The bells are used for country dancing as well as Morris dancing. They are worn to make the evil spirits happy.

3 The following questions are all about some of the other information contained in the recording.
   a) What sort of town is Shoreham?
   b) The dancers are called the Chanctonbury Ring Morris Men. What do you know about the Chanctonbury Ring?
   c) What do you know about Dick Playall?
   d) Has the Shoreham May morning ceremony been going on for long?
   e) Is there any connection between the wearing of bells by Morris men and church bells?
   f) What musical instrument is mainly used to accompany Morris dances?

4 Discuss and decide in your group which traditional ceremony in your own country is most similar to the May Day ceremony in Shoreham. Discuss the similarities and differences.

Documentaries

A visit to a sausage factory

Reason for listening

Most people from other countries think English sausages are rather strange. You might learn something about English sausages by listening to this documentary – but it is not intended to be very serious.

A visit to a sausage factory

After listening

1 Comment on the following statements.
 a) I've never heard of Trowbridge. There can't be anything important there.
 b) A banger is a firework, that's all.
 c) It's silly making people wear special hats in a factory.
 d) They ought to make men cover their beards as well.
 e) It must be a very small factory.
 f) I'm sure the ingredients in an English sausage are just thrown together without any proper control or examination.

2 Find out if your group can agree on the exact details of the 'sausage records' mentioned at the end of the documentary.

63

Documentaries

Wordlist

The mind's eye

braille   a system of writing and reading using raised dots on a page which makes it possible for a blind person to read with his/her fingers
access   way of getting to
travelogues   travel stories
plot   a story of a book
given in flashbacks   in a book or film where the time suddenly changes to an earlier period than the main events of the story
crude language   swearing; using rude words
foul-mouthed   using rude or dirty words
one man's book is another man's poison   a version of a popular proverb that says: 'One man's *meat* (i.e. food) is another man's poison', meaning we do not all like the same things
another facet   another side
panel   team or group
edited   they decide what to keep and what to cut out
track   the part of a tape that carries the recording
spools   the spool holds or contains the tape
playback head   the electrical device that 'reads' the recording and begins to turn it into sound
servicing volunteers   people, who are not paid, who help the organisation by repairing machines that go wrong
mailing list   list of people that an organisation writes to
bearing in mind that   remembering
the tricks of the trade   how to do something; things that make a job easier

May Day

May Day   May 1st
mingle with   mix with, go in together with them
portly figure   he is a bit fat
(to) process   walk in a procession
very widespread   you could find it almost everywhere
blacked their faces   put black paint on their faces
Moorish   from North Africa (once a common name in Britain for all people with black skins)

scare away, frighten away   put fear into them; make them afraid
sanctify   to make holy and safe from evil spirits

A visit to a sausage factory

mission   task, job
close to my heart   something I'm very fond of, like very much
get my teeth into   something I can really enjoy working hard at
gastronomic delights   very good things to eat
Mecca   the main centre
frightened out of their skins   terrified
crust   the pastry on top of a pie (*doing their crusts* means going crazy)
probing (questions)   searching questions to find out the true facts
shop floor   where the physical work is done in a factory
snood   net to go over the hair at the back of the head
facial (hair)   on the face
minced   cut into very small pieces by a machine
consumer protection department   government organisation to look after shop customers, i.e. people who buy things

8 STORIES

Drakesbroughton Hall

Reason for listening

Your only real reason for listening to this story is to be entertained and perhaps to be able to retell the story to someone else.

Drakesbroughton Hall

Listening

1 These questions are to help you remember the main points of the story.
   a) How long has the house been empty?
   b) Why has it been empty all that time?
   c) What is the house like now?
   d) Who was the last owner and what was he like?
   e) When did he inherit the house?
   f) What part of the house did he live in?
   g) What can you say about the room he lived in?
   h) What sort of people came to his parties?
   i) What had happened to him by the time he was 35?
   j) Who was at his last party?
   k) What happened at midnight?
   l) Did anyone escape from the house?
   m) What was the 'twist' at the end of the story?

2 When you tell a story like this it sounds better if you can give a few more details to add interest rather than just giving the main points. So can you supply any of this information...
   a) What do you know of the history of the house and the Wilkes family before 1767?
   b) What were the details of the central character's inheritance?
   c) Why does the house seem so silent?
   d) How many bedrooms could the last owner choose from?
   e) What was the date of his final party?
   f) What was his servant called?
   g) How exactly were you able to recognise the storyteller at the end?

After listening

Practise telling the story as though you were a visitor to the house and were shown round by the storyteller. What happened at the end and what did you do?

Stories

The interview

Reason for listening

The reason for listening to this story is to be entertained by a piece of good writing.

The interview

After listening once

There are a number of things in the story that would be interesting to talk about with other students.

1 Compare the initial reactions of the people in your group to the following:
   a) How happy do you think the central character really is?
   b) What do you think about her relationship with her husband?
   c) Is the 'formula' for love and marriage that Elizabeth Lightfoot presents correct and do you think that she is right in rejecting it?
   d) Is the interviewer's name significant?

2 Your discussion will probably raise some differences of opinion. So listen to the story again and see if you can resolve the differences.

Stories

The devil undone

Reason for listening

The reason for listening to this recording is simply to enjoy the story and perhaps be able to tell it to someone else.

Listening

1 Correct these statements if they are wrong.
    a) The storyteller was sitting in a restaurant.
    b) Where the present building is there used to be a grocer's shop.
    c) Zebediah was a cobbler all his life.
    d) His wife came from a wealthy family.

The devil undone

e) Zebediah went to another village to work.
f) He was 40 when the devil visited him.
g) He got his pot of gold seven years later.
h) He was 47 when the devil came back.
i) A horse kicked the devil back to hell.
j) When they built an inn they called it 'The Devil Undone'.

After listening

1 Fill in the missing words in this version of the story:

On the .... spot where the .... called 'The Devil Undone' now stands there used to be a .... shop where a man called Zebediah Bayliss lived and worked with his .... He was the son of a farm .... and worked on a .... himself before he became a .... He got .... when he was 19 and his .... never stopped .... about how .... they were. On his .... birthday Zebediah was at the .... of his .... Everything had gone .... that day and his wife had not stopped .... since .... He badly needed money. 'I'd .... my soul for a .... of gold,' he cried. Suddenly he saw a .... figure standing in front of him. It was the .... himself. 'I'll give you your .... of gold, Zebediah,' he said, 'if in .... years' time you give me your ....'

Zebediah was so desperate for money that he .... The .... disappeared and there on the floor was a great .... full of .... The .... and his wife lived .... from that moment. Zebediah only .... when he

71

Stories

 felt like it and his wife had nothing to .... about.

  .... years later, however, the .... appeared again.
'Are you ready to keep your bargain?' the devil .... Zebediah.
'Yes, I'm ready,' Zebediah replied, 'but first I would like you to give me one more ....'
'Very well,' .... the devil, 'but make it .... We have a .... way to go.'
Zebediah made his wish. 'I wish you were back in .... never to return!' he cried.

 With a crash the .... flew through the .... onto the back of an old .... which .... off at great speed.

 The .... never .... and Zebediah and his wife lived .... for the rest of their lives.

 When their .... was pulled down, the .... they built in its place was first called .... , but this later became changed to ....

2 Before the end of this week tell the story to someone who has not heard this recording.

Wordlist

Drakesbroughton Hall

haunted   a ghost walks there
panelling   thin pieces of wood covering the walls
rotting away   falling to pieces with age
sound   firm, strong
nest   to make a nest
grave   a hole in the ground that a dead body is put in
deranged   mad
sadistic   enjoyed being cruel and hurting people
crystallised   become fixed
legend   popular story
tomb   a place built to put a dead body in
inherited   received when his father died
scorned   had no interest in
altar   a flat-topped table used in religious ceremonies
paraphernalia   equipment
black mass   a religious ceremony by people who follow the devil
cronies   close friends
idlers   people who did no work
slab   large piece of stone
trap door   a door in the floor that opens upwards
quavering   trembling
lunatic   like a madman
brandishing   waving in his hand
sobered   they were no longer drunk
jagged   with rough edges
replica   copy
trident   a fork with three points
out of their minds   mad
insane   mad
ramblings   words that do not seem to make sense

The interview

medieval   from the period approx. 1100–1500 A.D.
faerie castle   a castle that looks as if it comes out of a traditional story book

envy   a feeling of anger and annoyance because someone has got something you have not
smudge   an indistinct mark (as you get if you pick up a clean piece of paper with dirty hands)
mug   large flat-bottomed cup or glass with a handle
churn out   produce automatically
neither here nor there   it is not important
scrapes a living   finds it hard to get enough money to live
on the hook   uncertain; waiting for a decision
off the record   not to be recorded
ungallant   not behaving as a man should to a woman (in a traditional romantic, polite fashion)

The devil undone

undone   defeated
legend   a popular story – probably not true
sinister   mysterious and frightening
cobbler   a shoe-maker and mender
labourer   worker
hedger   someone who makes or repairs hedges
mud   very wet earth
damp   feeling wet
jerkins   leather jackets
derelict   in a bad condition; almost a ruin
outskirts   on the outside of the village
this very spot   the exact place where we are now
grumbled   complained
whined   made complaining noises
incessantly   without stopping
many a time   often
vowed   promised
docile   he did not have the energy to move
capitulated   let the other side win
fate   destiny; whatever it is that decides what will happen to us
last   a shoe-maker's model of a foot
to crown it all   on top of all this
nagged   grumbled and found things wrong
daybreak   the beginning of the day

at the end of his tether   he had had too much; he was going to give up
cheered   made him feel happier
soul   spirit; the part of a person that in the Christian religion goes either to heaven or hell when he dies
fireback   the back of the fireplace
a pale blur   the outline was not clear
ransom   an enormous amount
dun   a greyish-brown colour

9 DISCUSSIONS

Violence in sport

Reason for listening

When you listen to a discussion like this you are usually interested to find out how the speakers' opinions agree or differ in relation to your own. There is also the possibility, of course, that the speakers might have an influence on how you think about the subject.

Before listening

1 Think about the question of violence in sport. Ask yourself and, if you are working with others, ask your group:

Do you think sport is getting more violent?
Are the spectators at sports competitions getting more violent? If so, why?

Violence in sport

2 Do *not* listen to the discussion yet. Answer these questions on your own. What do *you* think?

	Yes	No	Don't know
Are sports competitions good for international relations?			
Is playing the game more important than winning?			
Is violence among spectators caused by violence between players?			
Is the fact that some sports stars are paid a lot of money a reason for violence between players?			

Now listen to the recording.

After listening

1 How did the speakers' opinions compare with yours? Fill in the following table and compare the opinions expressed with your own.

Opinion	Did anyone agree? YES/NO	If anyone disagreed, write down what they said.
Sports competitions are good for international relations.		
Playing the game is more important than winning.		
Violence among spectators is caused by violence among players.		
The fact that some sports stars are paid a lot of money is a reason for violence between players.		

Discussions

2 Compare and discuss your results with the others in your group.

3 There may be some other points made by the speakers that you could use in a discussion of your own about this subject. Discuss and answer the following questions:
 a) What did they say about referees?
 b) What is Rugby Union a good example of?
 c) What has Rugby League got to do with the question of professionalism and violence?

Class in Britain and America

Reason for listening

When you listen to a discussion like this you are usually interested to find out how the speakers' opinions agree or differ in relation to your own. There is also the possibility, of course, that the speakers might have an influence on how you think about the subject.

Discussions

Before listening

1 Think about and discuss these questions.
   a) Do you have class differences in your country?
   b) If the answer to a) is yes, can you say how you decide what class people are in?
   c) Are people in your country divided in ways other than by class?
   d) Do you think the British can be separated into classes? If so, how?
   f) From what you know about America, do you think they have class distinctions there?

After listening

1 Consider the questions above again. Can you add anything to your answers?

2 Which of the following opinions would the American speaker probably agree with? What would he say about the opinions that he would NOT agree with?
   a) There is less class distinction in Britain now than ten years ago.
   b) There are three main classes in British society.
   c) Accent distinguishes American classes more than British ones.
   d) The upper class is the most snobbish.
   e) Middle class people hope to move up in society.
   f) Upper class people do not seem to care what they do or what people think of them.
   g) There is no point in trying to achieve equality of opportunity for all.

Sex discrimination

Reason for listening

When you listen to a discussion like this you are usually interested to find out how the speakers' opinions agree or differ in relation to your own. There is also the possibility, of course, that the speakers might have an influence on how you think about the subject.

Discussions

Before listening

1 Think about the question of sex discrimination. Ask yourself, and if you are working with others, ask your group:

   Should men and women be treated as complete equals?
   Do women still need to fight for fair treatment?

2 Do *not* listen to the discussion yet. Answer these questions on your own. What do *you* think?

	Yes	No	Don't know
Do women find it harder to get some jobs than men?			
Is a law giving equal rights to women a good thing?			
Should employers be allowed to advertise jobs for men only?			
Can changing the law change people's ideas?			
The person in charge of a meeting is called the *chairman*. If that person is a woman should she be called something else?			

Now listen to the discussion.

After listening

1 How did the speakers' opinions compare with yours? Fill in the following table and compare the opinions expressed with your own. Remember that speakers may give a strong indication of what they think without actually saying anything specific.

Sex discrimination

Opinion	Did anyone agree? YES/NO	If anyone disagreed, write down what they said.
Women find it harder to get jobs than men.		
A law to make people give equal rights to women is a good thing.		
Employers should be allowed to advertise jobs for men only.		
Changing the law can change people's ideas.		
The person in charge of a meeting is called the chairman. If that person is a woman she should be called something else.		

2 Compare and discuss your results with the others in your group.

3 There may be some other points made by the speakers that you could use in a discussion of your own on this subject. Discuss and answer the following questions.
   a) Does Jan think we should wait for things to change by themselves? Do you agree with her?
   b) How can you make sure a job advertisement is legal?
   c) Were all the speakers generally in agreement?
   d) Can you think of a non-sexist name for a person who is in charge of a meeting?

Discussions

Wordlist

Violence in sport

substitute   something you put in another thing's place
foment   increase
the be all and end all   the most important thing
professional foul   breaking a rule on purpose to prevent the other team or player getting an advantage
prevalent   it very often happens
responsible officials   the officials in football are the referees and the linesmen; they are responsible if they do their jobs seriously and well
the terraces   where the spectators stand to watch a football match
Rugby Union   a game with 15 players on each side played with an oval shaped ball that you can pick up and run with; the players are amateurs
tackle   an attempt to get the ball away from another player
bodily assault   a physical attack; an attempt to injure another person
sent off   told by the referee to leave the field because of a very bad foul
defuse the situation   calm things down
Rugby League   a game like Rugby Union but with 13 players in each team; they are professionals

Class in Britain and America

stratification   division into different levels
it pervades everything   you find it absolutely everywhere
Pygmalion   the name of a play by George Bernard Shaw (the basis of the famous musical show My Fair Lady)
strata   level or layer (as in stratification)
point-to-point   a horse race from one point in the countryside to another
parking lot   an American English expression for a car park
Range Rover   a type of British car made to travel across country as well as on the road (typically used by upper class people in the country)
hilarious   very funny
clan   a large family group, like a tribe; a group of people who are similar in many ways
the landed gentry   upper class people who own large areas of land
groom   a person who looks after a horse

paternalistic   acting like a father in a protective way
staggered   amazed; very surprised
tied cottage   usually a cottage that goes with a job on a farm (if you leave the farm you must leave the cottage)
off the top of my head   without having time to think properly
upwardly mobile   able to move up in society
uninhibited   not worrying about what other people will think about the things they do

Sex discrimination

gradual   slow
discriminated against   someone has been unfair, e.g. a woman is not given a job just because she is a woman
valid grounds   real reasons
unjustified   there is no good reason for it
stamp it out   stop it completely
interview   talk to people to see if they are right for a job
on equal terms with   in the same way as
draughtsman   a person who draws plans
it's implied   it makes people think that
chairs the meeting   is in charge of the meeting

10 TELEPHONE MESSAGES 2

See Unit 6, page 56, for the instructions on what to do.

TRANSCRIPTS

At the airport

Part one

Alitalia to Milan, flight number A2291 now boarding at gate 6. Alitalia flight number A2291 boarding gate 6.

Passengers to Madrid. Iberia Airlines of Spain regret to advise a delay of two hours on their flight IB551 to Madrid. This delay is due to the late arrival of the incoming flight. That is a delay of two hours on Iberia flight number IB551 to Madrid.

This is the final call for Air France to Paris, flight number AF814. Any remaining passengers must go immediately to gate 4 where the flight is now closing. Air France flight number AF814 closing now at gate 4.

British Airways to Tokyo, flight number BA5 now boarding at gate 2. British Airways flight number BA5 boarding gate 2.

Part two

Saudia to Jeddah, flight number SV172 now boarding at gate 4. Saudia flight number SV172 boarding gate 4.

This is the final call for Sabena to Brussels flight number SN608. Any remaining passengers must go immediately to gate 8 where the flight is now closing. Sabena flight number SN608 closing now at gate 8.

Passengers to Zurich. Swissair regret to advise a delay of 40 minutes on their flight SR805 to Zurich. This delay is due to a mechanical fault. That is a delay of 40 minutes on Swissair flight number SR805 to Zurich.

British Airways to Singapore, flight number BA11 now boarding at gate 6. British Airways flight number BA11 boarding gate 6.

Part three

This is the final call for Olympic Airways to Athens flight number OA260. Any remaining passengers must go immediately to gate 2 where the flight is now closing. Olympic Airways flight number OA260 closing now at gate 2.

87

Transcripts

Scandinavian Airlines to Stockholm, flight number SK528 now boarding at gate 4. Scandinavian Airlines flight number SK528 boarding gate 4.

Passengers to New York. British Airways regret to advise a delay of 35 minutes on their flight number BA175 to New York. That is a delay of 35 minutes on British Airways flight number BA175 to New York.

Austrian Airlines to Vienna, flight number OS455 now boarding at gate 8. Austrian Airlines flight number OS455 boarding now gate 8.

At a railway station

Part one

The next train to arrive at platform 2 will be the 15.02 to Newport calling at Filton, Severn Tunnel Junction and Newport. Passengers for Hereford change at Severn Tunnel Junction. Passengers for Gloucester change at Filton.

The 15.12 to Taunton, due to depart from platform 1 is reported running approximately 13 minutes late. We apologise for any inconvenience this may cause.

The train now standing at platform 4 is the 15.15 to Bath Spa, calling at Keynsham and Oldfield Park. The 15.15 to Bath Spa now at platform 4.

Here is a platform alteration. The 14.45 from Weston-super-Mare to Severn Beach, due in at 15.17, will depart from platform 3 not platform 5. The 15.17 to Severn Beach will depart from platform 3.

Part two

The 13.30 from Taunton to Cardiff due in at 15.20 is reported running 40 minutes late. Passengers for Newport and all stations to Cardiff are advised to catch the Swindon train leaving platform 6 at 15.25 and change at Bristol Parkway.

The next train to arrive at platform 8 will be the 15.23 to Bristol Parkway calling at Lawrence Hill, Stapleton Road, Filton and Bristol Parkway. Passengers for Montpelier and all stations to Severn Beach change at Stapleton Road.

The train now standing at platform 2 is the 15.27 to Taunton, calling at Nailsea, Weston-super-Mare, Bridgwater and Taunton.

The next train to arrive at platform 5 will be the 15.29 to Gloucester calling at Filton, Bristol Parkway and Gloucester. Passengers for Newport and Cardiff change at Bristol Parkway. Passengers for Hereford change at Filton.

News summary 1

Here is a summary of the news.
Shots are fired in a south London street by escaping bank robbers.
Four rock fans die in a stampede at a concert in Chicago.
And how an Air France Concorde was involved in the closest recorded miss in aviation history.

Shots were fired this morning in the course of an 80 m.p.h. chase along Brixton High Road in London. A police constable was injured by flying glass when a bullet shattered his windscreen as he was pursuing a car containing four men who had earlier raided a branch of Barclays Bank at Stockwell. Police Constable Robert Cranley had been patrolling near the bank when the alarm was given. The raiders made their getaway in a stolen Jaguar which was later found abandoned in Croydon. Officials of the bank later announced that £16,000 had been stolen.

Four people were killed and more than fifty injured when fans rushed to get into a stadium in Chicago yesterday where the British pop group Fantasy were giving a concert. The incident occurred when gates were opened to admit a huge crowd of young people waiting outside the stadium for the sale of unreserved seat tickets. People were knocked over in the rush and trampled underfoot as the crowd surged forward. The concert later went ahead as planned with Fantasy unaware of what had happened. A police spokesman said that they had decided to allow the concert to proceed in order to avoid further trouble. There has been criticism of the concert organisers for not ensuring that all the tickets were sold in advance. Roy Thompson, leader of Fantasy, said afterwards that the whole group was 'shattered' when they heard what had happened. They are now considering calling off the rest of their United States tour.

The United States Air Force has admitted that a formation of its fighters and an Air France Concorde recently missed colliding by as little as 10 feet. The Air Force accepts the blame for what was the closest recorded miss in aviation history. According to the Air Force spokesman, when the Concorde was already 70 miles out over the Atlantic, on a scheduled flight to Paris from Dulles International Airport, Washington, four U.S. Air Force F–15s approached at speed from the left. The lead plane missed the underside of Concorde's nose by 10 feet while another passed only 15 feet in front of the cockpit.

Forest fires in the South of France have claimed the life of another fireman as they continue to rage in the hills between Fréjus and Cannes. Fanned by strong westerly winds the flames are now threatening several villages and many holiday homes have had to be abandoned. The French army was called in yesterday to assist the fifteen hundred fire fighters that have so far been unable to contain the spread of the blaze.

A demonstration against race prejudice drew thousands of people to central London this morning. It was organised by the Labour Party and the Trades

Transcripts

Union Congress under the banner 'United against Racialism'. The march was led by several leading Labour Party and Trades Union Officials. It was a column that stretched for over two miles and it took the demonstrators nearly three hours to cover the distance from Speakers' Corner to Trafalgar Square. There were representatives from more than twenty major unions, as well as community workers and various ethnic groups. By the time the march reached Trafalgar Square an estimated fifteen thousand people had joined it.

Heathrow Airport Police are investigating how a mailbag containing nearly £750,000 worth of jewels went missing between Geneva and London. The mailbag was believed to be on its way to a London dealer from a jeweller in Geneva five weeks ago, but it was not realised it was missing until the Post Office reported the fact to Scotland Yard two days ago. The mailbag contained a diamond, an emerald and two rubies valued at £635,200 plus a number of stones of lesser value, according to a police spokesman at Heathrow.

Football. The draw for the semi-final of the F.A. Cup was made earlier today. Liverpool will play Manchester City while Arsenal will meet Nottingham Forest.

And that's the end of the news.

News summary 2

Here is a summary of the news.

No general election yet says the Prime Minister.
Five people die in an earthquake in central Italy.
And £$\frac{1}{4}$ million is stolen from a security van.

In a speech in the city of London last night, the Prime Minister announced that there will be no general election in the near future. Talk of a quick election was pure speculation, she said. A general election would be held when it was in the best interests of the nation to do so.

In central Italy, several small towns and villages are still cut off by avalanches following the earthquake during the night which killed five people. It was central Italy's strongest earthquake for several years and hundreds of people have been made homeless. In Rome, as well as in Florence, Naples and Perugia, gas pipes were broken, windows shattered and electric cables thrown onto the streets.

Thieves got away with almost £$\frac{1}{4}$ million after a security van was ambushed in central London early this morning. The security van was rammed by a lorry as it was taking a short cut through a narrow street off Piccadilly. Three masked men then threatened the driver and his assistant with shotguns and forced one of them to unlock the van. The thieves made their escape in a car parked nearby. This car was later found abandoned in south London. The driver of the van and his assistant were badly shaken but not seriously hurt.

Transcripts

The flight recorder of the DC10 airliner which crashed in the Antarctic a fortnight ago has shown that the plane was flying normally just before impact. All two hundred and fifty seven people on board the aircraft died when it hit the side of a volcano. The investigation into what happened is still going on.

Voting is taking place today in the Euro-Constituency of London South-West. This by-election for the European Parliament is being held because of the death of the previous member, Mr Harold Friend. At the last election Mr Friend had a majority of 17,000 over his nearest opponent.

Talks on a formula for ending the strike at Independent Television get under way in London this afternoon. Looking forward to the meeting, the General Secretary of the Association of Cinematograph, Television and Allied Technicians, Mr Albert Tapper, said it was taking place on the basis of new proposals from the companies. He hoped it would lead to a basis for negotiations but he refused to speculate on the chances of success.

Fifteen people are to appear in court in Manchester today following disturbances on a train bringing football supporters back from matches in London. Eye witnesses report that the trouble began when groups of rival supporters whose teams had both been playing London clubs began to insult each other. After fighting had broken out police boarded the train just outside Manchester and arrests were made. British Rail have announced that they are considering withdrawing all soccer specials operating from Manchester.

Short summary 1

Here's the news at 11.30.

Thousands of people have marched through the centre of Corby in Northamptonshire to protest against plans to close the steel works, the town's major employer. The marchers demonstrated outside the local British Steel Corporation's headquarters where union leaders are talking about closure plans with the management.

Hospital waiting lists in the south west of England have gone up by a quarter in the last five years. While the number of doctors, nurses and other staff have increased, the demand on the service has grown even faster.

The EEC is to give another £31 million to Britain's poorer areas. The aid from the regional development fund includes £13½ million for Northern Ireland and £10 million for industrial improvement and roadworks in the north of England.

In a report on rabies controls, Kent County Council has said that 17 dogs, 5 cats, 2 rabbits and 2 hamsters have been landed illegally at Channel ports in the first nine months of this year. This was seven more than in the same period last year.

Transcripts

A derailed coal train at Thirsk in North Yorkshire has disrupted rail services between Newcastle and the south of England.

That's all the news for now. Back to . . .

Short summary 2

It's time for the news at 3.30 here on Radio I.

A girl aged 16 armed with a shotgun held up a class of children at a secondary school in Surrey this morning. Police said that soon after school began at Blair Hill Secondary School, Newton, the girl, armed with a double-barrelled shotgun belonging to her brother, went into one of the classrooms and threatened a teacher and about thirty pupils. A shot was fired into the ceiling as she was being overpowered by police officers.

Surgeons at Cambridge have successfully transplanted a pancreas – the organ that produces insulin – in two patients suffering from diabetes. One patient, a 23-year-old electronics worker also had a liver transplant. The other patient, a 55-year-old housewife, had a kidney transplanted at the same time. Both patients are doing well.

A stately home owner who allowed a pop concert to be staged in his grounds was fined yesterday for letting a rock band play overtime. The Honourable Frederick Sidgwick-Johnson admitted allowing the rock group Led Zepplin to play on after midnight during a concert at his home near Stevenage two months ago. Stevenage magistrates fined him £125 with £25 costs.

Three people have so far been killed in the storms sweeping across the north of England and southern Scotland. A woman was killed in Carlisle when a chimney on a house collapsed and two men were killed when their car crashed into a fallen tree on a country road near Melrose. More high winds and rain are forecast for tonight.

Starting a new life

Nigel Fitz-Hugh: I came down here and then thought 'What can I do for a living?', and I started by selling dog beds or making dog beds, which sounds funny, but I invented a sag bag for dogs – a bean-filled cushion just like a human sag bag, but for dogs, you see. And I made one for our dog and thought that, and he thought that was good news and seemed to like it but whenever we took it around, all sorts of other dogs used to leap straight into it, and that was fine. And then I was down here with nothing to do. Well, I said, well we've got a house and my wife had just had a baby the day we moved into the house; and 'What can I do for a living?' I mean it sounds ridiculous looking back but I was so fed up with what I used to do that I was, I was desperate. And then I thought, well, I'll mail order these dog beds and see what happens. And I did, and for four years I was making dog beds in the garage and selling them; sending them out. Oh, a ridiculous amount of dog beds, just from the garage at the bottom of the garden. With me and a big pair of scissors and a sewing machine. And then, as I say, I was doing that and really making good money, I just, I just got itchy feet, I, I always have, I like a change; so as I was doing this I thought, 'What can I do? What else can I do? This is boring me.' Then thought, 'What can I do? What are my hobbies?' Well beer-making was one, mending clocks was another and making furniture was another. But so I thought, 'Well a lot of people make furniture, there are probably people who can mend clocks better than I can, but nobody's really, well not many people,' there was only one I could think of at the time, 'who've started a small brewery,' y'know? So I thought, 'Well that's er, good enough,' and it helps when you're doing a business on your own to do something that's different, er, gives you a head start, like the making of dog beds. There wasn't anybody else in it then but there are lots of them at it now. Er, but there wasn't anybody else in it and likewise this was different, so you could get publicity for a start. And it worked really well, it went off like a bomb, and er since starting this, I think every new brewer that's started up in the last year or two has, has been here one time or other, er, I, er, it's rather flattering in a way, I mean, a lot of them probably know more about it than me but it's nice to see someone else's venture even if you do know more about it than him. But um, if er, when people talk about a small brewery, I've probably met the guy and that's nice y'know, to know, to know, all these other people. So it's going well. And I sold the dog bed business to the chap next door and he's making dog beds now in the garage at the bottom of his garden. Actually that's not quite true, until, until two weeks ago he was in the garage at the bottom of his garden, and he just got a, found a bigger premises, a bigger factory and he's making dog beds. I dunno, there's so many people in it it's very difficult to, er, to keep it going well I think.

Female voice: You think you want to stay in brewing? You don't want . . .?

Nigel Fitz-Hugh: Yes, I do really, I feel I must. You know, I started this because I thought, 'Well, I can't go on making dog beds for life,' I don't, I don't see my future in dog beds. Er, but I think in a brewery, a small local brewery, you could establish and keep going for life. Cor it's a, it uses an awful lot of energy. Not not just physical energy but mental energy, keeping everything going by yourself. I should really have someone to help me but I just don't like working with people. Er, if there was someone working here with me and you get a sunny day, I think, 'Oh I've got ten minutes, I'll go out and sit out there and have a cup of coffee or something,' and if there was someone working with me I'd say, 'Get on with it, I'm just going out to do some sunbathing,' and I feel I, I, couldn't do that. So it's much easier to work by yourself, y'know, er work harder at it I suppose.

A weekend in London

Hello! I'm very pleased that you have decided to join one of our next London weekends. My name is Diana and I will be your resident guide during your stay in London. We shall arrive at the hotel at about 6.30 on Friday evening. Remember that we are staying at the Y Hotel in Great Russell Street – that's on the corner of Tottenham Court Road.

After you've got to your room and you've had a chance to freshen up, I hope you'll join me for a short walk through the West End of London. Leaving the hotel at 7.30 sharp I shall be strolling down Charing Cross Road, turning off through part of Soho to Piccadilly Circus, then through Leicester Square to finish up at Trafalgar Square. On the way we'll pass a lot of the restaurants, theatres and cinemas that you'll be able to visit during your stay in the capital.

The walk should take about half an hour and when we get to Trafalgar Square you'll be free to go off and do whatever you like. Why not have a quick meal and then see one of the latest films in one of the many cinemas around Leicester Square.

If you haven't stayed out too late on Friday night, please join me at 9.30 on Saturday morning for a walk through the great parks of London. We'll take a short trip on the underground to Lancaster Gate and stroll across Hyde Park to the famous Serpentine Lake (don't forget to bring a piece of toast from breakfast with you to feed the ducks). From there we'll cross over Hyde Park Corner, one of the busiest traffic intersections in central London, and make our way down Constitution Hill in Green Park to Buckingham Palace. If we can see the Royal Standard flying on top of the Palace we'll know that the Queen is at home, but I don't suppose we shall see her. From Buckingham Palace we shall cross into the third Royal Park of St James's – possibly the most beautiful of all, and we shall arrive at The Horse Guards in plenty of time to see the ceremony of the Changing of the Guard which takes place every morning at eleven o'clock.

On Saturday afternoon you might like to visit The Houses of Parliament, (remember they are only open to visitors on Saturdays during Parliamentary sessions). If there is some shopping you have to do, now is the time to visit the Oxford Street stores, or if you feel like relaxing on a boat for a while, you can come with me on a trip down the River Thames to Greenwich. I'll be at Westminster Pier (near The Houses of Parliament at 2 o'clock in the afternoon, so join me then if you'd like to visit the Maritime Museum and the Old Observatory at Greenwich and see some of the great River Thames at the same time.

Saturday night is theatre night and we shall have tickets available for either a top musical or a straight play. I'll give you details on Friday when you arrive and you'll be able to choose which you want to go to. On Sunday morning you have the opportunity to visit the great street market of London in Petticoat Lane. I'll be leaving the hotel at 10.30. You can buy anything from a tin whistle to a tiara in Petticoat Lane, so come and join in the fun. I'll take you to a traditional London pub for lunch afterwards and then it will be time to get back to the hotel, pick up your luggage and begin your journey home.

I hope I've given you a clear idea of the programme for your London weekend and before I finish let me just give you one or two pieces of advice which should make your stay more enjoyable. First, please do remember to bring with you some comfortable shoes to wear. London is a big place and whatever you do, you'll find yourself doing quite a lot of walking, so comfortable shoes are a real necessity. And secondly let me ask you to please look after your money. Keep it safe at all times and then you will avoid an unpleasant accident which could spoil your whole weekend. You'll find a summary of your weekend programme enclosed with this tape. Well, that's all from me for now. I look forward to seeing you soon. Goodbye for now.

Voices in my head

Narrator: It's a whole world that even partial deafness shuts off. I had an abscess in my left ear, and when it burst, it left behind a tiny scab that restricted the normal movement of my eardrum. Enough to make the noise of traffic recede, but with that went many other things. The real problem, though, was with people – suddenly I found they'd been talking to me and were expecting a response . . .
Female voice: When do you start your new job?
Narrator: And I had to get them to repeat what they'd said . . .
Female voice: When do you start your new job?
Narrator: And repeat it . . .
Female voice: When do you start your new job?
Narrator: . . . I don't know whether their annoyance was the law of the jungle despising weakness, or anger because they thought I was making a fool of them, or fear because they couldn't see anything physically wrong with me, like mental illness, but they treated me to a straight, unthinking cruelty just like a child does sometimes.
Child's voice: Are you deaf?

Transcripts

Narrator: At work, where life is competitive and you need to understand what people ask or require of you, I began to feel stupid when I missed the odd word and found I couldn't understand what was being talked about. Mind you, people don't articulate much at the best of times.

Female voice: I beg your pardon?

Narrator: They don't ar-ti-cu-late.

Male voice: A ticket inspector came into a compartment of the London to Brighton express and he found the only passenger tearing up his newspaper and wadding up the single sheets and throwing them out of the window. 'What are you doing that for?' he says . . . (*background noise increases – voice becomes indistinct*)

Narrator: It was the laughter, I couldn't stand being outside the laughter. I felt isolated, and that's when I began to feel I was being isolated; was even the subject of the laughter. There were hostile looks when I missed a change of subject in a conversation.

Female voice: Is he really stupid or is he just being bloody rude?

Narrator: So I opened my mouth less and less, used the pose of a vacant abstracted smile for a time and then withdrew from conversations almost completely. I was left on my own, out on my own. And that can get more than just depressing . . .

Voices: There are voices . . ces . . ces . . ces . . . there are voices . . . There are voices in my head . . avoid . . avoid . . ces . . ces . . dead . . dead . . .

Narrator: During this time I was an outpatient at a throat, nose and ear hospital in London. Everyone kept saying:

Female voice: Go and see a specialist.

Narrator: But I hesitated, partly because someone who was a specialist was already treating me and partly because it's difficult to know who to choose without a recommendation from someone personally. In the end, thank goodness, that's what happened and I got the second opinion.

Female voice: It's worth a fiver just to know.

Narrator: In fact, it *is* worth it. Nothing too drastic showed up, but after a week or two, the improvement in my hearing was marked. It wasn't just a door opening, it was that I could hear the door opening.
Being able to communicate properly with people again did wonders for my self-confidence. It wasn't just words, it was the tone and texture of a voice, the grunts, the breathing, the verbal gestures – all sorts of subtlety I'd been missing – things you need when people mumble and mutter and swallow their words as much as they do. They're part of language as well. (*sound effects*) It was all music to me; I was part of the human race again.

Male voice: . . . the only passenger tearing up his newspaper and wadding up the single sheets and throwing them out of the window . . .
'What are you doing that for?' he said.
The passenger said, 'I'm keeping the elephants off.'
'But there are no elephants,' said the ticket inspector.
'I know,' said the passenger, 'extremely effective isn't it?'

Show jumping

- Paul Tiles goes through the start and safely over the first which is the famous Cornishman, that's the safe brick wall
- Oh, he stood right back at the second and he ploughs through the oxer, fence number two, so that's four faults so far for Springtime as he turns down the far side and straightens up towards fence number three
- Goes down by the side of the tennis court fence, one of the permanent fences here
- Jumps the gate, fence number three
- Now he'll go down towards the Derby Bank
- He doesn't jump the Derby Bank in this
- He goes towards fence number four, which is three upright poles over a six foot wide ditch and that's full of water
- Clear over that, four faults at the moment
- As he goes round the back of the Derby Bank
- Comes back towards us
- Towards the next fence which is a rustic
- Rustic natural poles
- Oxer
- Sails over the top of that
- Nice chestnut horse Springtime as he comes towards the planks – upright fence – right down the side of the arena
- Lot of cars over that side
- Now he comes towards the double
- Just towards us now
- A double of oxers
- Safely over the first
- One stride and safely out over the second part
- Now he turns left-handed
- He's halfway round
- He's got four faults at the moment as he swings away from us
- Goes down the arena towards fence number eight which is the rustic triple bar
- Clears that with a good foot to spare
- Steadies himself because the next one is the upright
- There are about twelve yellow and white poles very high upright, sails over the top

- He's down in front of the Derby Bank on the far side which looks very green incidentally here in the rain at Hampton
- Now he turns right-handed
- Comes up towards the next fence
- This is the combination fence
- And he's got that all wrong
- And he's all wrong for the second but recovers well and safely out over the third part
- Hit the first part
- So that's four faults there, so eight at the moment
- He comes down towards the second last
- This is the water
- Sixteen feet
- Clears that with a good two feet to spare
- Steadies himself
- Going a bit too fast for the upright but jumps it clean
- And that's not a bad round for Paul Tiles on Springtime
- Eight faults
- Gets a well-deserved round of applause

- The next to go is Fred Scott on Dartmoor, and he's safely over the first
- The Cornishman
- Fred Scott going for his second clear
- He's already clear on True Girl
- Safely over the second fence, the rustic oxer
- Now turns right-handed
- Goes down by the side of the tennis court fence and straightens up towards fence number three
- This is the gate
- This is the one that Maureen Ford had down
- Fred Scott jumps it clear on Dartmoor
- This horse I've seen jump over seven feet at Olympia
- Won the Puissance at Olympia
- And sails over the top of the open ditch on the far side
- Now he goes round behind the Derby Bank
- He reappears and he'll straighten up towards fence number five which is the oxer, right on the far side
- We're stretching ourselves to see if he can jump this clear
- Yes, he can
- Coming down by the side of the arena with all the cars parked there
- And all the cars are packed out today
- With the heaters on no doubt and perhaps a few of them listening to this commentary on the radio in their cars

- Safely over the planks, the upright
- Now towards the double
- Jumps the first part
- Lifts him over the second
- Clear halfway round
- Fred Scott on Dartmoor
- Four clear so far
- Fred's been at the top for many years now
- Must be round about fifty
- I've always asked him his age but he hasn't given me the same answer twice
- It varies between the ages of 21 and 22 but believe me he's well over 50
- But he's a superb
- Oh, he's got the upright down
- What a shame
- He was going so well and the yellow and white polled upright on the far side has come down
- And that's four faults for Dartmoor
- Now he turns right-handed up in front of that open stand on the far side
- Where there are still a few people
- Safely over the first in the combination
- Jumps the second
- That's gone
- Safely over the third part and the ground out there getting progressively worse, more sticky as the competition goes on with all the divots that these horses are throwing up
- He's in the water as well, yes, up goes the flag
- Twelve faults as he comes down towards the last
- Fred Scott stands back and Dartmoor jumps it clean
- But twelve faults for Dartmoor

Football

- Ten minutes gone in the second half here
- Liverpool 1–Manchester United 1
- Liverpool bidding to reach their fourth F.A. Cup Final in eight years
- Manchester United bidding to reach their third final in four years
- Marvellous cup traditions these two have
- As Bailey kicks a long ball down field into the Liverpool half
- It's cleared, it's gone out of play in fact for a throw-in
- Halfway inside Liverpool's half on that far side
- Arthur Albiston, who played so well in the Cup Final two years ago when he came on to replace Houston for United when United beat Liverpool takes the throw
- Receives the return ball

Transcripts

- Prods it to the edge of the Liverpool penalty area
- It's half cleared but back in it goes again it's
- There's a goal
- Is it?
- Yes
- Manchester United have scored
- Brian Greenhof gives them the lead
- It was a clumsy sort of goal but Brian Greenhof won't worry about that
- Liverpool *will* worry because now
- And it hasn't happened often this season
- They find themselves 2–1 down
- The ball knocked in by Albiston
- It came out again
- Jimmy Greenhof played it back into the box
- It seemed that Liverpool had to get it clear
- There seemed no immediate danger
- And then Brian Greenhof moved in quicker than any Liverpool defender and hit it home
- That could be such an important goal
- Manchester United 2–Liverpool 1
- Now is the moment when the young players in this somewhat inexperienced United side will really come of age
- And now is the moment when the vast experience of Liverpool will be tested to the full
- They're 2–1 down in the F.A. Cup semi-final
- Will it be United going to Wembley and will their jinx over Liverpool work again
- And I notice that the Liverpool substitute Heighway warming up on the touchline so perhaps Bob Paisley's ready to play his ace
- But Liverpool go forward with Ray Kennedy
- Just outside the United penalty area
- He's tackled
- The ball spins loose
- What a dramatic comeback by United
- Hughes for Liverpool
- Halfway inside United's half
- Lobs it into the penalty area
- Kennedy's on the end of it
- Goes down but not fouled
- The goal kick to Manchester United

- We've got a cup-tie and a half here
- We've got eight minutes to go

Transcripts

- Manchester United 2–Liverpool 1
- It could be about 5–3 at the moment
- A tremendous cup-tie and Liverpool have a corner
- Again Dalglish will take the corner on Liverpool's left to the near post
- Thompson goes in
- He's gone up for the corner
- It's cleared through by United
- Hughes gets underneath it
- A loose ball from him but Souness is on to it
- Turns back to Neal
- Still inside his own half
- Clemence now is standing three yards outside his own penalty area urging his side forward
- McDermott
- Thompson tries the shot
- Bailey
- It's there
- Alan Hansen has got it for Liverpool
- Alan Hansen the tall Scotsman playing in his first ever semi-final
- Not so long ago playing for Partick Thistle
- Well it's Alan Hansen's first goal of the season and Liverpool have gone totally mad over that one
- He was there when it mattered
- Good running by Heighway
- And Liverpool have come right back here
- Seven minutes to go
- Liverpool 2–Manchester United 2

- It's boiling inside the United penalty area now
- We're in injury time
- As Coppel comes forward for United himself
- Jimmy Greenhof
- Hansen's alongside him
- Greenhof checks his stride
- Good tackling by Ray Kennedy there down the line
- And Heighway's on-side
- Heighway's on-side and he's going inside United's penalty area
- He has a look
- He'll cut it back
- A good ball laid out to the far side
- McDermott tries the shot
- It cannons off a defender
- I don't think people can bear to look out there at the moment

101

Transcripts

- It's 2–2 injury time
- McDermott wants to take the throw quickly for Liverpool
- Finds Dalglish
- Overhead kick from Dalglish
- He's looking for Johnson
- Can't find him
- The ball is cleared
- Neal comes thundering up through for Liverpool
- Lays it square
—Ray Kennedy
- Kennedy good intelligent ball finds Hughes
- He's on the edge of the United area
- Hughes brought down I would have thought
- And it is a free kick to Liverpool
- And this could be the last assault here for Liverpool
- Fourteen years of course in Europe
- They're used to tension and pressure Liverpool
- This indeed is their twelfth F.A. Cup semi-final
- As they play the free kick to Heighway
- Heighway across the United area again
- Good defensive work by McQueen
- Coppel goes back to help
- That's the whistle
- And it's a shame that it's over
- A marvellous semi-final here
- And in the end it's deadlock
- 2–2
- And it has to be done all over again at Goodison Park

Horse race

- Any second now they'll be under starter's orders
- They're all in
- Up goes the flag
- They're under starter's orders
- Away they go
- A very level break, Rhyme Royal broke very quickly indeed and he's making the early running
- And it's Rhyme Royal from Palimon and Jellaby
- These are the three who broke fastest from the stalls and they're setting a terrific pace down the back straight with Palimon out in front of Rhyme Royal
- In third place Jellaby
- Then Sexton Blake and Effulgence then Swiss Maid and Fluellin last at the moment

- And they're really stretched out as they go past the mile point
- With Palimon taking them on
- Right behind him is Rhyme Royal being rousted along by Willie Carson
- A length and a half then to Jellaby
- Then another length to Sexton Blake
- Then Effulgence half a length away
- Then Swiss Maid and Fluellin bringing up the rear of the field as they go to the railway turn, right down the far end of Sandown with the rain still pouring down here
- And Palimon has the lead by a length and a half from Rhyme Royal still being ridden along to keep second place
- Jellaby in close touch third
- Sexton Blake very much improving on the outside who is a very close fourth
- Then Effulgence, Swiss Maid and Fluellin
- They're rounding the far turn
- And Palimon still out in front by a length and a half from Rhyme Royal who is the same distance in front of Jellaby
- Sexton Blake is just going on the outside of Jellaby to dispute third place
- Then behind Jellaby on the inside Effulgence then Swiss Maid and finally Fluellin and they're turning into the straight
- And it's Palimon and they're swinging right wide and coming right across onto the stand rails
- And the leader Palimon and they're all following him
- Palimon from Rhyme Royal then Jellaby then comes Sexton Blake and Effulgence then Swiss Maid and Fluellin
- Three furlongs out and it's still
- Now Jellaby comes storming through to take over in the lead
- Palimon drops away quickly
- And Jellaby, last year's winner of this race
- From Rhyme Royal and Effulgence and Sexton Blake
- Sexton Blake with a lot to do
- Then comes Swiss Maid
- They're coming to the last two furlongs
- And the long stride of Jellaby is surely going to tell here
- Jellaby and Rhyme Royal together
- About three lengths clear of Sexton Blake
- Who's under pressure and making no headway
- They're into the last furlong now
- And it's big brave Jellaby
- Still running on strongly with Pat Eddery
- Rhyme Royal doing everything he can to get on terms
- A two horse race
- And Jellaby is the stronger of the two
- And Jellaby's going away from Rhyme Royal and Sexton Blake and Effulgence

- And Jellaby wins this race for the second time
- By three parts of a length from Rhyme Royal
- Another five lengths before we come to Sexton Blake
- Another good six lengths before Effulgence
- Then Swiss Maid, Palimon and Fluellin

David Attenborough

Interviewer: Which area, of all the ones that you've visited, is your favourite?

Attenborough: Oh, I find that almost impossible to answer really. Um you know, different places for different things. The South Seas are a pretty divine sort of place to be, you know, I mean Fiji, the islands east of there; the people are so charming and amazing. Er, and then I'm very fond of South East Asia because it's got such wonderful past; it's got so many temples buried in jungles and so on. And the Galapagos Islands with fantastic birds and reptiles. I don't know, it's very difficult.

Interviewer: I wonder what makes you come back to England?

Attenborough: Well, as a matter of fact, of course that's the trick isn't it? I mean you, almost anything, I think, change like happiness is er, no change produces happiness in many ways. I mean, it seems to me that happiness has something to do with changing. The happiest times are when you're always just about to do something, when you've just moved from this to that, er if you then actually get into a situation and it doesn't change, after a bit, er the happiness part begins to wear off and I don't know whether that's a limitation in human beings but I think it's true. But in fact, you don't actually have the op . . you don't have the option really, do you? Because actually life is always changing, people around you are changing, you're getting older, emotional things change, and so on.

Interviewer: Before all this you were on the management side of the BBC, in fact, for eight years. How did this part of your nature, didn't you feel very frustrated because you really wanted to be a creative artist?

Attenborough: Well, I think that's what I was saying about change really. I think um, new things, new challenges, that's a corny phrase for you, but nonetheless, they are very important and if someone, if you care about making television programmes, or if you care about making radio programmes, and someone says to you 'Oh, by the way, old boy, er, we've got, er, a new network here and there's twelve million quid or twenty million quid or whatever it is, we're not quite sure actually what to use it for, but perhaps you could think up a few programmes if you'd like to go away and spend it.' Er, you have to be a very funny sort of broadcaster if you don't say 'Well, thanks very much, I'll start tomorrow.' And if after two years they say 'Oh, by the way old boy, because of the technical characteristics of the network you're running, you will be the first colour network in Europe, so we want you to think how perhaps colour should be used.' Well, you again have to be a very funny television producer to say 'I'm not interested.'

Interviewer: I'm still interested in what you say about change. Do you feel that anybody has the power to create this change within their lives, um or do you think that some people can't help being absolutely bogged down in whatever their particular path is?

Attenborough: Well, what I mean is that, that, er, there are two elements in that. Of course the world changes around you and therefore you are changed, I mean you get older, so you change, er you meet different people, so you change, er you produce children and they change you and they grow up and they leave and yet again you're changed. So that you are changed willy nilly by the forces around you. But you also have it within yourself to bring about change, er and you, you set yourself targets, it seems to me, that 'Oh, I wish I could do this; I wish I could own my house; or I wish I could play the piano; or I wish I could grow geraniums; or, or whatever.' And, and the change that comes and brings the joy and the satisfaction is that you actually do those things and you achieve those things. And, of course, if there were actually only so few, that you never wanted to change anything then, I think, you'll be a great deal will be missing from your life, a great deal of pleasure.

Mrs Victor Bruce

Interviewer: I'm going to talk to you now about the suffragette movement. Were you yourself ever a suffragette?

Mrs Bruce: No, I did not approve of suffragettes. I did not want to have the vote. I felt the man of the house should be in charge of that section. And the woman, of course, to look after the home and the children. I think that voting was unnecessary, at that time. But I'm not going to say now, that perhaps it has had its advantages.

Interviewer: How common was your attitude at the time that the suffragettes were being militant?

Mrs Bruce: Oh, I was very much against them. I'd be highly insulted if anybody called me a suffragette. I remember walking with my governess down Downing Street just past Number 10 and they chained themselves to the railings. Of course, I had a good laugh but I thought it wasn't going to be me.

Transcripts

Interviewer: Were they a popular movement in their day?
Mrs Bruce: Well, with a certain number of course. And they tried very hard and eventually they got the vote, er through their efforts, so I suppose their efforts were good in quite a lot of ways. Er, I think women in Parliament – there aren't many, but those that've been there have done a lot of good.
Interviewer: So you think in the long term . . .
Mrs Bruce: In the long term, no harm was done. As long as their demonstrations were peaceful.
Interviewer: Do you think it would matter very much if women didn't, hadn't achieved the vote, if they hadn't got the vote at all and still didn't have it?
Mrs Bruce: I don't think it would've made a great deal of difference, no, but there are certain things they've done – those that've been Members of Parliament – that have been very useful in helping women in their jobs, in other vocations. I think it's good that it happened. But I wish it happened a little bit more peacefully, perhaps.
Interviewer: What sort of things can you remember, what other sorts of demonstrations do you remember?
Mrs Bruce: Marching, they were marching. But of course those were much more peaceful days, nobody interfered with their marches. There were a few boos here and there and a lot of clapping. Yes.
Interviewer: Did you, did you actually know any suffragettes yourself?
Mrs Bruce: Well, my friends, my close friends, were not suffragettes but I had one or two friends, not very close friends, that were. And we used to have great arguments and I used to say I didn't want the vote, I don't want to vote.
Interviewer: How did they react to that?
Mrs Bruce: They didn't like that. They said I ought to join the movement but I said, no I don't want to vote.
Interviewer: But, and yet you've done so many exciting things. You've done so many things that in your day, were probably the exclusive preserve of the man
Mrs Bruce: Well, yes. But voting didn't make any difference because that's a political thing, voting, I never, I don't care about women entering into politics particularly. Ah, no harm's been done with the few that have entered the House of Commons but, in fact, some have done a great deal of good. But that's quite different to beating men at their own job. Now that's nothing to do with votes. Now, for instance, I always got a great thrill on the race track at Brooklands, if I could beat, well, Sir Henry Seagrave, for instance, in a race, I never did beat him but I did beat Frazer Nash, a famous racing driver in a race, and I was thrilled to death. I thought that was super.

Interviewer:	So you don't mind actually joining men in their world of work and sport but you're happy to leave politics to them.
Mrs Bruce:	No. I would rather really leave politics to them.

Renee Wyndham

Interviewer:	How many different countries do you think you've been to?
Wyndham:	Once I made a count of how many countries I'd hitchhiked through and it came to twenty eight. So if you add on a few more for those where I haven't hitched, I imagine it comes to about forty by now.
Interviewer:	About forty! And are there any of these that you feel you really would like to go back to?
Wyndham:	Two that I could actually live in I think. One would be the west coast of Canada because I think that had everything to offer. It was rich culturally, it was very bright, it had a very pleasant climate, slightly improved on Britain. It had the Rocky Mountains behind, loads of coastline, um, a lot going on both day and night, a large university, and it was just near America if you felt like crossing the border. The other place I liked, but more for a holiday, was Sardinia, which I found was one of the quietest, most unspoilt parts of Europe that I've seen.
Interviewer:	What is it about travelling that makes you want to keep doing it?
Wyndham:	I think it's the one time when I feel completely alive every minute of the day. I also feel I have a tremendous amount of experience to bring back every time I've travelled, there's so much to share with other people. I feel I've got, sort of, two hundred per cent me to give once I come back. But when I'm actually doing it, you're you're free from all the bounds of routine, you're free from the assumptions people make about you. You're free from the inhibitions that cause you not to fully be yourself and enjoy yourself because of what people might think and so on.
Interviewer:	But it can also be a little bit dangerous at times too, can't it?
Wyndham:	It can certainly be dangerous if you're doing it alone. I avoid travelling alone wherever I can. I mostly go with people I know very well and this is part of the travel er discovering the person you're travelling with and discovering the differences in taste and the similarities in taste. But, um the most dangerous situation I found myself in was nearly being knifed here in Devon, in Ilfracombe. But apart from that, I was on a train in Hungary where there was a murder in the loo, and we were kept for 10 hours while they investigated why somebody had been stabbed in the loo. I've also slept, voluntarily, in a prison in Norway and another prison in Germany. Um and in one of them we were locked in and heard the other prisoners shouting and banging on the doors and that felt

Transcripts

Wyndham: quite frightening. Um I managed to get right into the centre of the Middle East war through no choice of my own. They wouldn't let us out of the plane and we were caught throughout the whole war in the country and couldn't get around at all. That felt as if you were living on a knife edge; we were lying there contemplating quite coolly whether, if there was an air raid, we should actually go into the shelter or allow ourselves to be killed on the spot. And, er there are certainly risks and I think more so when you do travel alone, so I try and avoid it.

Interviewer: Mm. But travel is er is quite an expensive business too, isn't it? How do you afford all this gadding around the world?

Wyndham: Well, a large part of it is through my main work, travel is really a side occupation – a very pleasant one – my main job is broadcasting. But apart from that, you don't need an awful lot of money. I've found that you can live much more cheaply in other countries, sometimes, than you can over here. Also a lot of my really good friends have places in, scattered all round the world, where they're very kind and put me up and I try and reciprocate and so on. And you can live very cheaply, eat very little, rough it, sleep in hostels, sleep out, walk to most places, hitchhike and give concerts when you're on the spot. I do a lot of singing and entertain the natives and also give concerts lately that seem to give me enough money to spend several weeks living off the proceeds. Um the broadcasting I do in this country, again, I'm lucky enough to have short contracts and projects, which means that when I've done a few of these or just a series like I did recently for Radio 3 which was repeated, um the money comes rolling in after a while and I save it all, gather it all together and take off somewhere else.

Interviewer: Mm well, good luck and bon voyage!

Wyndham: Thank you very much, David.

Michael Parkinson

Interviewer: With all your experience of interviewing, Michael, how can you tell if somebody is going to make a good interviewer?

Parkinson: Oh, I say, what a question! I've never been asked that before. Um I think that the prerequisite obviously is is curiosity, I think that's the er a natural one, not an assumed one. I think the people who have um done my job, and the graveyard of the BBC is littered with them, their tombstones are there, you know, who failed, have been because basically they've not been journalists. Um, my training was in journalism, I've been 26 years a journalist and, er to be a journalist argues that you like meeting people to start with, and also you want to find out about them. So that's the prerequisite. After

	that, I think there's something else comes into it, into play, and I think again, most successful journalists have it, it's a curious kind of affinity with people, it's an ability to get on with people. It's a kind of body warmth, if you like. If you knew the secret of it and could bottle it and sell it, you'd make a fortune.
Interviewer:	When you've done an interview yourself, how do you feel whether it's been a good interview or not a good interview?
Parkinson:	I can never really tell er on air. I have to watch it back, because television depends so much on your director getting the right shot, the right reaction you can't, it's amazing. Sometimes I think 'Oh, that's a boring interview' and just because of the way my director shot it, and shot reaction, he's composed a picture that's made it far more interesting than it actually was.
Interviewer:	How do you bring out the best in people, because you always seem to manage to, not only relax them, but somehow get right into the depths of them.
Parkinson:	By research. By knowing when you go into a television studio, more about the guest in front of you than they've forgotten about themselves. And, I mean that's pure research. I mean, you probably use, in a 20 minute interview, I probably use, oh, a 20th of the int . . . of the research material that I've absorbed, but that's what you've got to have to do. I mean I once interviewed Robert Mitchum for 75 minutes and the longest reply I got from him was 'yes'. And that . . that's the only time I've used every ounce of research and every question that I've ever thought of, and a few that I hadn't thought of as well. But that really is the answer – it's research. When people say to you, you know, 'Oh you go out and wing it' I mean that's nonsense. If anybody ever tries to tell you that as an interviewer just starting, that you wing it, there's no such thing. It's all preparation, it's knowing exactly what you're going to do at any given point and knowing what you want from the person.
Interviewer:	And does that include sticking to written questions or do you deviate?
Parkinson:	No, I mean what you do is you have an aide memoire, I have, my . . my list of questions aren't questions as such, they're areas that I block out, and indeed, I can't remember, I can't recall, apart from the aforesaid Mr Mitchum experience, when I've ever stuck to that at all. Because, quite often you'll find that they spin off into areas that you've not really thought about and perhaps it's worth pursuing sometimes. The job is very much like, actually, a traffic cop, you're like you're on point duty and you're, you know when you're directing the flow of traffic, well you're directing the flow of conversation, that's basically what you're doing, when you're doing a talk-show, in my view.

Transcripts

Interviewer: Have you got a last word of encouragement for any young people setting out on what they'd like to be a career as an interviewer?

Parkinson: I, I, envy them, I mean, I really do, I mean I'd go back and do it all again. I think it's the most perfect job for any young person who's got talent and ambition and energy. And the nice thing about it is that the proportion of talent is indeed only 5 per cent. The other 95 per cent is energy and no examinations to pass. I'd love to do it over again.

Telephone messages 1

Woman: Look, I've only got a moment so will you give Horatio a message for me please? Tell him I can't see him tonight, but I'll be at the usual place tomorrow. O.K.? Thanks very much. Goodbye!

Man: Look, I can't stop. Tell Horatio I couldn't get the red ones, but there are plenty of blue. He can see them any time. Oh, my name's Ted. Bye!

Man: Tell Horatio something for me, will you? Tell him Helen is furious about the mix-up last Saturday and she's after his blood. He'd better ring her or something. Got that? O.K. Cheerio!

Woman: Will you give Horatio a message as soon as he comes in, please? Tell him Helen called. Tell him I think he's a worm and I'm waiting for an apology. That's all.

Man: Well, I was hoping to speak to Mr Hamilton myself, but perhaps you'll give him a message for me. Tell him that Mr Evans of Smith and Wheeler called. There are a few details regarding the sale of his property that we need to discuss and I'll be glad if he would contact me as soon as possible. Thank you very much. Goodbye!

Woman: Oh! Well, will you tell him Rebecca called? Give him this message. Remember your promise. That's all. You will do that, won't you? Don't forget. Bye!

The mind's eye

Voice: The mind's eye.
Man 1: To be absolutely honest, I've never heard of it.
Woman 1: I've seen something about it on the telly.
Man 2: Yes, I have heard something about it.
Man 3: Yeah, well, it's er, it's er, oh, I dunno.
Woman 2: Yes, I have read something about it in the papers.

Woman 3:	Talking books? No. What are they for?
Female voice:	What are they for? If only she knew. But do you know what a talking book is?
Male voice:	It is not generally appreciated that less than 20 per cent of blind people can read braille. Therefore the only access to literature, for the vast majority of blind people, is through the talking book. And we here in the Royal National Institute for the Blind have designed this specialised equipment, which is the first equipment which was designed specifically for use by the blind. And here we have every form of recorded literature that you could find in a public library. Travelogues, histories, thrillers, biographies, the Bible, everything.
Female voice:	All books aren't suitable for reading aloud. Some have too much dialogue or a plot given in flashbacks to the past make it difficult to follow. Other books have too many foreign words, or diagrams, statistics and, of course, crude language.
Female voice:	That reminds me of the lady who returned a sea story to us only half read. 'Never in my life,' she wrote 'would I allow such disgusting language in my sitting room, and I'm not having that foul-mouthed man in here now!' Of course, one man's book is always another man's poison. As I said, it's a question of balance, of trying to supply books for all tastes.
Female voice:	But who records the books? Well, this is really a matter for professional readers, and even among them, some selection is necessary.
Female voice:	Some books have got a lot of characters in them. Some readers are very much better at characterisation than others. And therefore, you wouldn't give a book full of characters to what we term a straight reader, who reads an autobiography or that sort of thing perfectly.
Male voice:	Another facet of this programme is the student library. It had been felt for some considerable time that many blind students would benefit if we could provide them with their various technical books in recorded form. And we've now established a panel of voluntary readers around the country each with their own tape machine. We provide the tape and the printed book and our volunteer readers record these books in their own home. The books, when they've finished recording them, are sent back to us here in Great Portland Street and are edited.
Female voice:	Now we have the edited tapes from both professional and volunteer readers and these are taken to the library at Alperton.
Male voice:	We do three things really. We make copies from the original tape, we store the finished copies or cassettes on the library shelves, and we organise the distribution of cassettes and the issue and

Transcripts

	maintenance of the machines themselves. Our tape is half an inch wide and has 18 tracks. A tape and two spools and a playback head are all enclosed in the cassette. When the user puts the cassette on the machine, the connections to the head are made and the spools are driven at constant speed. At the end of each track, the cassette has to be turned over and the head moved down to the next track. This is done automatically by pressing a button, and there are only three controls – start/stop, volume and the track change button.
Female voice:	This is where the chief recording engineer comes in.
Male voice:	As there are eighteen tracks, the original tape has to be divided into 18 sections of approximately equal length. And yet each break must be in a sensible place. What we have to avoid is this sort of thing . . .
Actress:	John darling, come and sit beside me here. Darling . . .
Female voice:	That is the end of track seven, please turn the cassette over and press the button once.
Female voice:	Now you may be wondering what happens if something goes wrong. Well, all that is organised too.
Female voice:	Here in Alperton we have one thousand six hundred servicing volunteers on our mailing list. Bearing in mind that there are at least twelve thousand members of the library, it can easily be seen that we need many more volunteers in many parts of the country. Every morning when the mail is opened, we receive many requests for assistance and also telephone calls come in during the day. Our response to this is to notify the nearest volunteer and ask him to go along and visit the reader.
Male voice:	We also go along when a new member gets a talking book and spend an hour or two showing them the tricks of the trade.
Male voice:	Right, let's put it on this little table between us and we can go over it together. That's right. Now give me your hand. Er now, you'll feel at the back of this platform there are two projections. These locate the cassette and you just put it down on the thing. Don't bother about it, it'll fall into place. That's it.
Female voice:	Like that?
Male voice:	That's right. That's it! Now at the front there's a knob that turns the whole thing on and off. And then there's a little . . .
Female voice:	Here?
Male voice:	Yeah, that's it. Now there's a little lever up here that starts the tape. Now push that away from you.
Female voice:	Like that?
Male voice:	That's right. (*male voice reading on the cassette*) And then you can make it louder or softer with this connection.
Female voice:	Oh, yes.

Transcripts

Male voice: And that's all there is to remember.
Female voice: Oh, that's quite simple isn't it?
Male voice: Absolutely simple.
Female voice: I wouldn't be without it. It's one of my most treasured possessions.
Female voice: Well, if I have a very interesting book, I can't let it go. I go on to 11 o'clock at night sometimes.
Male voice: I'm doing the Bachelor of Science in Economics at the present time and I'm taking the Part One in two weeks' time.
Female voice: One can't travel, so one does it by reading.
Female voice: I just must finish it. Sometimes I have it so quietly, that so that people don't hear and it's sometimes half past eleven, when it's very interesting.
Female voice: You can knit and listen to that, and you can't read braille and knit can you?
Female voice: Oh, it is a tremendous help. I don't know what I should do without it now.

May Day

(*music*)
Narrator: These are the sounds that you can hear just after sunrise every May Day in the streets of Shoreham, a small harbour town on the Sussex coast. Traditional celebrations for the coming of summer mingle with the sounds of Morris dancers, in fact, the Chanctonbury Ring Morris Men, named after that circle of trees planted on the South Downs in commemoration of Queen Victoria. Well, one of their dancers, with over 20 years' experience, is Dick Playall, his portly figure filling his gaily decorated, but traditional costume, he looks and sounds just like a Morris man ought to.
Playall: I think probably Shoreham is only one of relatively few places in the country where they do have a May morning celebration. I mean we have been doing this for about 20 years now, without missing a year. And we go down to the Coronation Green and then we have the crowning of the May Queen, May Queen, Shoreham May Queen um and we have dancing down there, then we process through the streets and er, to do some dancing at one or two other places and we come back here to St Mary's Hall and we have a May breakfast. (*music*)
  Morris dancing must have been very, very widespread throughout the country. But in many areas it, um died out, during, probably the, I don't know, nineteenth century with industrialisation. We haven't actually got very much tradition in Sussex for this. They did used to do what they called step dancing, um, which um, I suppose you could

Transcripts

call it a sort of Morris dancing. But the ones we do, mostly, are from the Cotswolds. This is a traditional English form of folk dancing. Originally the men blacked their faces because they were supposed to be anonymous, you see, they weren't dancing as themselves, they were representing, if you like, you might say, the sort of spirit of Spring and so on. And they didn't really, um it wasn't a good thing for them to be recognised. Probably because they blacked their faces they were called, it was called Moorish dancing and therefore, for Moorish became Morris, but no one is absolutely certain. (*music*)

Yeah, but of course the bells are only worn for the Morris, they're not worn for country dancing. It's like church bells really, you see they're to scare away the evil spirits. You know, you might think that the church bells ring in order to tell you that it's time for the service. In fact the church bells really are to sanctify the area, to frighten away all the evil spirits. As far as we're concerned of course it helps with the dancing because it all adds to the colour and sound of it. (*music, applause*)

A visit to a sausage factory

Announcer: We sent Tom Brown on a special mission. His destination – a town somewhere in Wiltshire and his task – to investigate the mysteries of the sausage.

Tom Brown: New York has the Empire State Building; Rome has the Colosseum; Paris has the Eiffel Tower and the Pompidou Centre. But Trowbridge, Trowbridge has Bowyers. Yes I've come here to Trowbridge, early on a grey January morning, to investigate a topic close to my heart – or rather close to my stomach – something I can really get my teeth into. Behind me is the Bowyers factory. I'm about to go through this gateway of gastronomic delights, to visit this Mecca of the meat pie. What's going on inside, I wonder? Are innocent sausages being frightened out of their skins? Are meat pies doing their crusts? I'm going in to talk to Mr Cook, the site manager, to ask some important, probing questions. Why are sausages called bangers, for instance?

Mr Cook: No, I'm sorry, I don't know. No, I don't know, no.

Tom Brown: I've noticed that everyone in the factory seems to be wearing a different kind of white hat.

Mr Cook: Well, everyone in a food factory has to keep clean and tidy and cover all the hair of the head. You will be putting on a hat such as the operators on the shop floor wear which is a white peaked hat with a snood down the back to cover all the hair on your head.

Tom Brown: Yes, I see it's got a rather fetching hairnet at the back. What's, what's the reason for that?

Transcripts

Mr Cook:	Well, to stop any hair falling out and landing up in a product. To keep it clean. I see you've got a beard, Tom, and at one time, you would've had to wear a snood over that as well, er, we don't do that any more because in fact, um facial hair doesn't come loose in the same way as head hair does.
Tom Brown:	Well, we're going over to the factory now to have a look at the production of food here. How many sausages do you produce every day here?
Mr Cook:	Approximately 110,000 pounds a day.
Tom Brown:	Right, well we're inside the factory now, in the room where the sausage-making process starts off and I've got Norman Brewer with me, who's the assistant manager here. Could you tell us what's going on here?
Mr Brewer:	Fifty per cent of the material used is basically minced and processed and sorted out before it actually goes to the chopping machines. It's pre-weighed before it goes to the chopping machines and everything is quality controlled and examined before the process is started. After the material has been mixed and chopped, as you can see, it's in a sausage form now, and er it then goes to what we call filler machines or stuffing machines. The sausages come through the stuffing machine and then they are twisted by another type of machine and then it goes to the wrapping stage, where it is inspected before it's wrapped and it's also checked for weight when it is wrapped.
Tom Brown:	I've always wanted to ask this in a factory that produces sausages. Do you know why a sausage is called a banger?
Female voice:	Probably 'cause they split in the pan.
Male voice:	And go bang.
Female voice:	I don't know, and go bang, yeah.
Male voice:	At a previous employer in the north of England we in fact made a sausage which, for a variety of reasons, we called a banger. Um in fact the local consumer protection department got very upset about this, that er we were not to call it a banger, we had to call it 'a something sausage'. Because a banger isn't just a sausage. It could have been an old car or it could have been a firework and they felt there might be some confusion.
Announcer:	There's more to sausages than meets the eye, it seems. I never knew sausages were so complicated. Did you know that the longest sausage in the world was 3,124 feet long and was made on the 29th of June 1966, and if you really like statistics, by 30 butchers in Scunthorpe. And the sausage-eating record is $89\frac{1}{2}$ Danish one ounce sausages in three minutes by Lee Hang of Hong Kong.

Transcripts

Drakesbroughton Hall

Narrator: So glad you could come. And welcome to Drakesbroughton Hall. This is the home of the Wilkes family, or it was until the last member of the family – Cornelius – died here 200 years ago. The house was built in 1587, rebuilt in 1690. It's been empty since March 1767, 200 years ago. Empty for 200 years. And why? Well, because Drakesbroughton Hall is haunted.

This is the Great Hall where, I suppose you could say, many people entered but few departed. The panelling's nearly all gone and the staircase is rotting away. The floor is sound, for few people have entered the Hall since 1767. There are no rats and no birds nest in the roof. There is an air of evil in this house and a silence of the grave.

Cornelius Wilkes, the last of a long line of evil and deranged men, was probably one of the most evil and sadistic men who ever lived. The stories of his goings-on are crystallised in legend and story, and it's difficult to know where truth ends and imagination begins. But perhaps, perhaps you'd like to hear about Cornelius Wilkes, as we go through this great tomb of a house.

When Cornelius was 25, his parents died, some say it was the wish of the devil and well it may have been. Anyway he inherited this great house, 400 acres of land, a cellar containing over 2,000 bottles of rare wine, 20 servants, 5 carriages and a great deal of money.

In this room, Cornelius Wilkes lived, ate and slept. He scorned the 20 great bedrooms and set himself up in this huge panelled dining room. The vast curtains remained closed, night and day. And here on this stone base was an altar, and on the altar was all the paraphernalia of Black Mass.

Cornelius gave vast and frequent parties for all his cronies – idlers, drunkards and no-goods. But all were rich and all were weak. The winds of hell blew round the Hall at night and can still be heard on the anniversaries of his more evil parties. Stories were told of Cornelius's communion with the devil and here, behind the altar slab, is a trap door which, it is said, led directly to hell. By 1767, Cornelius was 35 years old. For ten years he'd been living like a madman but now his money, his wine and his lands had all gone. Gone too, were many of his friends in the manner of rats deserting a sinking ship. Cornelius looked 50 with the eyes of a madman. He developed, in moments of stress and excitement, a quavering voice, and a stammer which he could scarcely control and which ended in lunatic laughter.

On the 11th of March 1767, Cornelius Wilkes gave his last party. His remaining five friends came at dusk to consume the last few bottles of wine. There was one servant – a man called Lancelot Sargent. The six of them drank until midnight and, as the clock struck the hour, Cornelius swayed to his feet brandishing an empty bottle. With a terrible cry, he threw the bottle at the black altar. His friends watched in sobered horror. As the bottle smashed on the altar a mighty clap of thunder crashed through the room. A jagged fork of lightning streaked out from the altar, piercing Cornelius through the heart. Cornelius Wilkes was dead. He lay on the carpet and on his face was burned a replica of the devil's trident. His friends, out of their minds with fear, ran for the door, but they never reached the safety of the world outside. One by one, they dropped and it was nearly 12 months before anyone could understand the insane ramblings of the servant Lancelot. And when the Hall was broken into, there was no sign whatsoever of Cornelius Wilkes or his five friends.

Perhaps you'd like to see upstairs, it's really quite in-interesting, r-r-rather interesting, I, I, er let's go up this way. I say, what are you staring at? What are you staring at? Oh, I see, I see, I see, you've seen the marks on my face, haven't you? Yes, you've seen the marks on my face. Well, well, well . . .

The interview

Am I happy? . . . You know, you're the first person to have asked me that question directly. The others never dared. The other interviewers, I mean. They never dared because they were frightened I might say 'Yes'. And they wanted the answer to be 'No'. They would come with their tape recorders and their notepads, take down everything I said, then go home and patch it together. 'Elizabeth Lightfoot, author of over 100 romantic novels, translated into more than 30 languages, with world sales topping the ten million mark, lives in solitary splendour in the medieval village of St Paul, some 20 miles inland from Nice. From the windows of her "faerie castle", she looks out at the distant blue of the Mediterranean and dreams up yet another best-selling romance. But is she happy?' And so on, and so on . . . That's why I stopped giving interviews. I'm tired of being told that because I'm rich and successful, I must be unhappy. I am *not* unhappy. Whatever they may think. Envy. It's all envy, really . . . Shall we move over to the window-seat and have tea? I shan't offer you anything stronger. I never drink during the day – it brutalises the brain. And very little at night. An occasional glass of wine with Harry over dinner. He's allowed two glasses. No more. He grumbles, of course, but he knows it's for his own good. None of my heroines drink. None. Nor my heroes. They have their own inner strength, you see. That's their appeal . . .

. . . There! Isn't that a wonderful view? That grey smudge to the left, that's Nice. It's perfect up here. Just far enough away to be free from the crowds, yet close enough to get into town whenever you need. Harry goes down every day. I don't really approve, but it keeps him out of the house. Work, he calls it. He's in the property business – buying and selling villas. . . . Do sit down. I'm terribly sorry, I've forgotten your name . . . Patricia? One of my heroines was called Patricia.

I hope the tea's not too strong. The flavour's so delicate, so easily spoilt. You don't take milk, I hope? Aren't the cups lovely? Eighteenth century. Harry drinks from a mug. Barbarous habit! . . . You were asking earlier if I write to a formula. That was a wicked question, but I know what you mean. Do I simply mix the same ingredients – castles and carriages, banquets and balls, candlelight and soft caresses – change the names, find a title, and churn out another romance? The answer is no. My heroines *live*. They think for themselves. They may live in the past, but that's neither here nor there. To take just one example: *Castle Keep*. That book alone has sold over 500,000 copies. And why? Not because it follows a formula but because it *breaks* a formula. The heroine, Sylvia, has two admirers – I never use the word 'lovers' – one rich, the other poor. The rich one owns an estate, which he wants to improve, to make even more profitable. The other, the poor one, is a musician, who scrapes a living by giving piano lessons to the children of the richer families. Sylvia, of course, is one of his pupils. She is admired by both of them, and returns their admiration. But which does she marry? . . . No, not the poor music teacher! That would be the formula. And it's the formula most women follow in their lives. They choose the weaker man, because they think he must be stronger in spirit; the poorer man because they think he must be richer in feeling! My heroine was right. She chose the man who could make her happy. The man who could shape his life, give it direction. What happened? The rich admirer built up a successful estate, and the poor admirer – instead of writing the great music he had promised – went on and on giving piano lessons . . . You see, I don't write to a formula. That story is drawn from life. My own life. When I was a young editor on Woman's Own, I had two admirers. One was Harry, of course. The other, a young music student called Mark. Strange, I can't even remember his second name. Something short. Harry was rich, Mark was poor. Harry knew exactly what he wanted: to work in the property business. Which he did, and very successfully. Mark never really knew what he wanted – to play, teach, compose, conduct . . . 'Something to do with music', that was all I could get out of him. Well, I kept them both on the hook for three years. By the end of the three years, Harry had already started his own company; Mark was still teaching music in the local school. And probably still is, for all I know. Oh, he had fine dreams of the music he would make. He talked wonderfully, but he never got round to making it. He wasn't a failure, but he didn't have that will to win. You know what I mean? That look you see sometimes in the faces of tennis players, when they grit their teeth and you know they won't be beaten – or at least they'll go down fighting. If I had married Mark, I'd have been dragged down by his failure . . . This is off the record, you understand? I've never told it to anyone. You're not to use it in the interview . . .

Ah. That must be Harry. I'll get him to drive you down to the airport. It's been *so* pleasant talking to you, Patricia. Next time, you must tell me something about yourself . . . Oh, Harry, this is Patricia . . . I'm terribly sorry, I still don't know your second name. Bell? Really? I was saying you would drive her down to the airport. Yes, I know you've just got back, but she has a plane to catch . . . Don't be so ungallant, Harry! . . . No, no, my dear. It's no trouble at all. He's just gone to wash his hands. He'll run you down . . . Bell? What does your father do? . . . A conductor? Bus or orchestra? Ah . . . No, I haven't heard of him. I don't go to concerts much. I don't suppose he's heard of me either. Success is always one-sided, isn't it? . . . Anyway, give him my regards when you next see him. Oh, and don't forget to send me a copy of the interview, will you? Just for the record.

The devil undone

Narrator: 'The Devil Undone'. Quite an unusual name for a pub, isn't it? Actually, it's not the original name. Nor, for that matter, is it the original building. Er, for according to legend, anyway, the original name, and the building, were a good deal more interesting and, for that matter, sinister. For, many, many years ago, the village cobbler's shop stood here. Not that that's particularly interesting, but the cobbler, and the events surrounding him at the time, were.

Zebediah Bayliss was born in the village, the son of a farm labourer, and inheritor of nothing. He married, at the age of 19, the daughter of a hedger, a dull girl of no charm, no wealth, and no ambition for herself or her husband. Zebediah worked on the squire's farm. He was a poor worker and longed to be away from the mud and the damp which affected him in the winter. Eventually, out of necessity, he took to repairing boots and jerkins. And in course of time became quite expert in the trade. On his thirtieth birthday, Zebediah obtained, for the sum of two shillings and four pence a week, the use of a derelict cottage, on the outskirts of the village; this very spot.

Life was not easy, Zebediah worked hard and long; he grumbled and, most of all, his wife grumbled. There was insufficient money, the cottage was damp and his wife whined and grumbled incessantly. And many a time Zebediah vowed to leave the village, but his dull and docile nature never permitted it. It was on his fortieth birthday that Zebediah nearly capitulated to fate. It had been a day of trouble – he'd spoiled a pair of boots, he'd cut his hand, his best last had broken, and to crown it all, his wife had nagged and whined, from the moment she had dragged herself complainingly out of bed at daybreak. Zebediah was at the end of his tether. And had it not been for an unpredictable and astonishing flash of brilliance in his dull and foggy brain, this pub would not have the intriguing name that it has.

For on the 20th of February 1727, Zebediah Bayliss called out to the devil. It was a dark, wet night. Zebediah had been working all day and he was very tired. Through the door from the shop he could see

his wife. He could see her mean little mouth working as she grumbled at her tasks, he could see the bright glow of the fire and smell the fresh bread in the oven. And none of these things cheered Zebediah.
'I wish to hell I'd got a fine, big pot of gold. Oh, I do that. I'd sell my soul for a pot of gold.' How unwise of Zebediah. For there, across his shop, stood a stranger, dark in the shadows, his clothes black as the fireback, his face, a pale blur, greenish in the light of the lamp.
'Zebediah, how nice of you to call me!'
'Who, who are you?'
'Oh Zebediah, come now, you said, you said, you'd sell me your soul.'
'Sell my soul? Why you're the Devil!'
'Oh, Zebediah, please, such language! A pot of gold you said – is that what you want? All right, Zebediah, if you promise to give me your soul at the end of seven years, I'll give you your pot of gold.'
'All right, Devil, all right.'
And at Zebediah's feet was a bag. A bag, which when tipped up, spilled forth a ransom in gold.

Zebediah and his wife lived comfortably. There were no more quarrels. Zebediah had no need to work so hard. People had to wait to have their boots, and wondered how and why a humble cobbler could be so independent. The years passed by and seven years to the day, on Zebediah's forty-seventh birthday, the devil appeared again.
'Ah, 'tis you Devil.'
'Yes, Zebediah. Time is up. Seven years, you remember.'
'Ah, I remember.'
'Are you ready then?'
'I'm ready Devil, but there's just one thing.'
'What is it Zebediah?'
'One further wish.'
'Oh. This is most irregular.'
'Er, just, just one.'
'Well, as you've been so gentlemanly about our, er, contract, I think I might grant you one more wish. But make it simple, Zebediah. And quick, for, for we've got a long way to go.'
'Right then, are you ready?'
'Make, make your wish, Zebediah.'
'I, I wish, I wish you in hell and never to return.'

And the devil disappeared with a crash through the window. He flew out into the field and landed on the back of an old dun cart horse, who was so startled that he set off at a tremendous gallop and was never seen again. Well, Zebediah and his wife lived on. Most of the gold which Zebediah had put aside he now used to retire upon and the couple lived happily for many more years. And when the cottage was eventually pulled down, to be replaced by an inn, they called it 'The

Devil upon Dun' which, in course of time became 'The Devil Undone', which is, of course, well, just as appropriate. Um, scotch please.

Violence in sport

A: Yes, people used to say that er sporting competitions between nations was a good substitute for war but it seems in recent times at football matches that it's er that they're taking war with them into the er into the football ground. I mean, does . . doesn't international competition in this way simply foment nationalist feelings and make the whole situation rather unsporting in the end?

B: I think it does, yes. I mean . . I . . er in a good game of um any sport really that . . I personally think if it's played as it should be played, winning is not the be all and end all, it's er playing the game . . which is the . . .

A: But is that possible today in a professional sport?

B: No, I'm afraid it isn't.

C: No, I don't think it should be in a professional sport. In a professional sport we're talking about winning . . um because winning is where the money is, hence professional and . . .

B: That's the way it is. Whether it should be is another question . . I er . . .

C: Oh no, that is how it should be. If you don't want it to be like that then you have amateur sport.

A: Well, what about the effect on the supporters though in that case. There . . is there any truth in saying that the violence on the field of sport between professionals who are behaving professionally and we've got this very unpleasant expression 'a professional foul' in football, doesn't that lead to violence off . . off the . . .?

C: Yes, I'm sure it does, and really we're talking about responsibility and I don't think that in some of the games where violence is prevalent, as for example football, that we have responsible officials. I think, er to stop violence on the terraces then, yes you must stop some of the violence on the field.

A: Maybe professionalism is part of this. I mean the . . perhaps the most violent game that we play in Britain on the field is Rugby Union and yet it's very rare for any, for there to be any er trouble in the grounds where . . .

B: The point is that in Rugby Union one can't tell the difference between a legitimate tackle and a bodily assault.

C: No, but I think that it's handled more . . more responsibly. For example, I believe in Rugby when one person is sent off, generally there's . . there's someone from the opposing side also sent off, and I think it's fair to say that in most er trouble spots there . . there is more than one person involved. By doing things like that you defuse the situation.

B: I think the referees in Rugby are much tougher. I mean, one . . one word against the referee in Rugby and you're off in a lot of cases.

Transcripts

A: But also, of course, it's an amateur game. There isn't the money in it is there, for the players.
B: But even in Rugby League where there is money involved, although perhaps not such a large extent on the whole as in football, the referee usually has much more control of the situation.

Class in Britain and America

Christine: Harry, as an American, have you noticed any strong class distinctions in English society since you've been here?

Harry: Strong class distinctions? Yes, they haven't changed at all – that's what – that's what amuses me – in fifteen years – or fourteen years – that the stratification is exactly the same as it was when I first came. It's extraordinary that it pervades everything.

Anna: What is class distinction? Because I don't know whether it's what job they do or . . .

Harry: It's people's accents. In Pygmalion, you know, it goes back to, as soon as you open your mouth in England you're immediately you know placed.

Anna: Do you mean that there aren't different accents in America?

Harry: Not – of course there are different accents – but they're not as – they're not nearly as clearly defined.

Anna: But I mean, don't – doesn't a certain strata of American society use perhaps more slang than another one? More correct?

Harry: Not the way they do in England. In England they seem to really stick together. I mean I went the other week for the first time in my life to a point-to-point and I couldn't believe what I found. There I was in the middle of Lincolnshire and we went through muddy fields and suddenly we came upon this parking lot with nine thousand Range Rovers in it and everyone going 'Oh, hello darling. How are you?' you know and it was hilarious I mean and they were all you know this meeting of the clan and that certainly doesn't happen in America and all those people spoke the same way.

Barrie: But that – yes, I live in the middle of the country in the south and I must say when I moved there I noticed – I mean of course I'd been aware of class before that but I had no idea that the lines between them were so rigid. I lived on an estate of a very big and successful farm until recently, and so the farm of course was run by the landed gentry who all went hunting and to point-to-point and all the rest of it. I lived next door to the groom who was – who despised them because they did all this and he had to just get the horses ready, um but at the same time he was terribly fond of them and they of him and there was all this sort of paternalistic attitude to the country workers that still goes on. I was staggered and nobody knew where to put me

	because I was living in a tied cottage that was tied to the farm, um but because I didn't work with any of them they were all uneasy with me. Most peculiar.
Christine:	But I think you raise a very good point there Barrie because you're in fact talking about yourself not fitting into either of these two extremes and I'd like to ask Harry again how many classes he can see very clearly defined.
Barrie:	In England?
Christine:	In England, yes.
Harry:	Well, I guess, three off the top of my head. I mean not counting immigrants and foreigners. Yes, I mean there's the middle class is the most snobbish of all it seems to me. You know, they're the most aware of the whole system really because they're upwardly mobile usually you know they hope to be, and they're the ones – I mean the upper class are what I find extraordinary – they seem to be totally uninhibited for the most part. I think it's extraordinary. I mean I'm not passing any moral judgements on them but it still exists . . .
John:	Because they've got the confidence . . .
Anna:	. . . and the money . . .
Barrie:	. . . confidence and the money . . .
John:	Well no, I don't think money's much to do with it actually.
Anna:	How can you change it? I mean how would you change it?
Harry:	I'm not saying it should be changed . . .
Anna:	No, no, no, no. I don't – I mean people do say that it should be changed. Politicians say that we should have total equality which I don't believe you can ever have in anything.
Harry:	Well there should be equality of opportunity. I mean at least it's a nice ideal to have, isn't it.

Sex discrimination

Jan:	Changes are very gradual. They're too slow. I mean if you sit under a tree long enough the apple'll fall off and you can eat it but sometimes you've got to stand up and do something. You've got to . . Um I think the law is there to protect people. Because women were being discriminated against, it was necessary for the law to stop that, um at least to some extent. But you can't change the way people think.
Duncan:	People's discrimination is based on the fact . . a lot of it, that they don't think women are capable of making decisions or have any intelligence at all. I mean a lot of people believe that . . and if that . . provided . . once that's proved wrong, that removes the valid grounds for the discrimination and you know you . . the belief is then unjustified. You've got to stamp it out. I mean, it's as simple as that.

Transcripts

Keith: But just in the same way that if I want to become a managing director, I have to look at the company in which I work and prove certain elements of my behaviour or . . or my skills to these people, so must women.

Jan: Yes, but if they're not given the chance, then how can they? I mean it's very sad that the law has to be there at all. I mean that you have to say to somebody who's employing someone you must give . . you must interview men and women . . it it seems a great shame . . you have to tell people to do that. It's also a great shame that you have to tell people not to go around murdering other people. I mean, the law's there because people do stupid things.

Duncan: As I say, the law is . . is not that you have to sort of . . I mean you basically all you have to do is give women the right to apply and the right to be considered in the same way as everybody else and if the law was effective as it should be, there'd be nothing wrong with that. I mean, what's wrong with giving women the chance to apply for a job and giving them the right to be considered on equal terms with men.

Keith: Women could always . . women could always apply.

Duncan: That's not true, though. I mean there are employers who just would not consider them.

David: A woman would not apply if the job was . . if the job advertisement was couched in such terms.

Keith: I mean . . the leading example . . .

Duncan: I mean the whole point about the . . an advertisement asking for a draughtsman being against the terms of the act, is that it gives the imp . . it's implied that only men will be considered and that's why that would be a legal advertisement if you put at the bottom, um applications from men and women will be considered . . the same with postmen and all the other jobs.

David: Interesting point. How important is the language, Jan, do you think?

Jan: I . . it's symbolic. Um I personally don't find it particularly important. Er if you have a meeting and you call the man or the woman who chairs the meeting the chairman, it just doesn't matter I don't think at all.

Telephone messages 2

Man: Oh! It's rather important, so could you give him a message as soon as he comes in? Tell him Jeremy rang to tell him that Harold Scott is retiring at the end of the month so there will be a job going if he's interested. O.K.? Thanks very much.

Woman: Oh dear! It's terribly important. Tell him I must talk to him before I go to France tomorrow, will you? I'm getting the 10.25 from Victoria but I'll be at home until about 9.30. Don't forget! It's very important!

Man: Will you make a note of a few details, please? Horatio will want to know this when he gets back. Tell him Smith and Harris definitely will, Simpson and Brown won't, and no one knows what Thompson will do. He'll understand. That's all. Thanks!

Woman: Oh! Well, will you tell Horatio that if he's still interested, it's at 8.30 tomorrow morning at the Astor Hotel. Jack and Marjory will definitely be there. Thanks!

Man: Out? What on earth is he doing? Well, when you see him, tell him that Thompson is hopping mad and he'd better get in touch with him as soon as possible.

Woman: Oh! Well, look, I've only got a second so I can't explain properly. Tell him Mary rang. Ask if he remembers Paris last April. If he does he can ring me today or tomorrow between 5 and 6 at 303-2345.

KEY

At the airport

Announcements are made in the following order in each part of the recording.

Part one

Alitalia	AZ291	Milan	Gate 6
Iberia	IB551	Madrid	2 hrs delay
Air France	AF814	Paris	Gate 4
British Airways	BA5	Tokyo	Gate 2

No announcement made for:
Sabena   SN608   Brussels

Part two

Saudia	SV172	Jeddah	Gate 4
Sabena	SN608	Brussels	Gate 8
Swissair	SR805	Zurich	40 mins delay
British Airways	BA11	Singapore	Gate 6

No announcement made for:
Olympic   OA260   Athens

Part three

Olympic	OA260	Athens	Gate 2
Scandinavian	SK528	Stockholm	Gate 4
British Airways	BA175	New York	35 mins delay
Austrian Airlines	OS455	Vienna	Gate 8

No announcement made for:
Lufthansa   LH067   Stuttgart

At a railway station

1 Platform 4.
2 No. The train was not announced as stopping there. (Perhaps you could change at Filton and get a train from there.)

Key

3 Filton.
4 Yes.
5 Yes. Change to platform 3.
6 Approx. 15.25.
7 It is probably a good idea to get on. Passengers will be getting off just down the line to change at Filton and Bristol Parkway.
8 Yes. At Stapleton Road.
9 Yes. But change at Filton.
10 Now. It is standing at platform 2.
11 Yes. Your train is delayed so take the 15.25 to Swindon and change at Bristol Parkway.
12 Yes. The 15.25 to Swindon stops at Bristol Parkway. Go to platform 6.

News summary 1

A 1 Four U.S. Air Force F-15s and an Air France Concorde.
   2 Seventy miles out over the Atlantic from the United States.
   3 The U.S. Air Force's. (They accepted the blame.)
   4 Dulles International Airport, Washington.
   5 Five.
   6 Ten and fifteen feet.

B 1 Chicago.
   2 The sale of unreserved seat tickets for a concert to be given by the pop group Fantasy.
   3 People were knocked over in the rush and trampled underfoot.
   4 Four people.
   5 To avoid further trouble.
   6 Because they did not sell all the tickets in advance.
   7 We do not know yet. Fantasy are considering what to do.

C 1 Forest fires are burning.
   2 Fifteen hundred fire fighters.
   3 The French army.
   4 Probably not.
   5 It seems not. It is still spreading.

D 1 Some bank robbers.
   2 Robbed a branch of Barclays Bank at Stockwell.
   3 A bullet shattered his windscreen.
   4 A stolen Jaguar.
   5 £16,000.
   6 They abandoned it in Croydon.

Key

Other news items
1 The draw for the semi-final of the F.A. Cup was made earlier today.
2 It told them that their teams would play Manchester City in the semi-final of the F.A. Cup.
3 The demonstration against race prejudice.
4 About fifteen thousand.
5 UNITED against RACIALISM.
6 They may be the jewels that were stolen between Geneva and London.

News summary 2

A 1 Independent Television.
   2 This afternoon in London.
   3 The TV companies.
   4 We do not know. (He refused to speculate on the chances of success.)

B 1 It was taking a short cut.
   2 They rammed it with a lorry.
   3 Yes, with shotguns.
   4 Almost £$\frac{1}{4}$ million.
   5 They were badly shaken but not badly hurt.

C 1 No, it was after the matches; on the way home on a train.
   2 No, they had been playing different London clubs.
   3 Groups of rival supporters began insulting each other.
   4 Police boarded the train to stop the fighting.
   5 British Rail may withdraw all soccer specials operating from Manchester.

D 1 Yes. Gas pipes have been broken, windows shattered, and electric cables thrown onto streets.
   2 Last night.
   3 The earthquake caused avalanches.
   4 Five people.
   5 Yes, hundreds of people have been made homeless.

Other news items
1 a) A fortnight ago in the Antarctic.
   b) No.
   c) It is not yet known.

2 a) Not in the near future.
   b) Because people had been talking about a possible quick election.
3 a) The European Parliament.
   b) Because the previous member died.
   c) Yes, he had a majority of 17,000.

Key

Short summary 1

You will use your own words in this activity, but your answers in the conversation should contain the same *information* as in these model answers.
1 Yes, they were demonstrating against plans to close the steel works, weren't they? (Outside the local British Steel Corporation's headquarters.)
2 Well, they're talking to the management about the closure plans.
3 Yes, they're giving another £31 million.
4 No, £13½ million is going to Northern Ireland.
5 Yes, they've brought in dogs (17), cats (5), rabbits (2) and hamsters (2) in the first nine months of this year.

Short summary 2

You will use your own words in this activity, but your answers in the conversation should contain the same *information* as in these model answers.
1 Yes, he let a band play on after midnight. He was fined £125 with £25 costs.
2 Yes, in Cambridge they've just transplanted pancreases in two patients. One of them had a liver transplant and the other a kidney transplant at the same time.
3 Yes, terrible, weren't they? Three people were killed.
4 Well, the weather forecast says there'll be more high winds and rain tonight.
5 Yes, a girl went into a classroom and threatened the teacher and the children with a shotgun.
6 Well, she did fire it actually, while the police were overpowering her. But the shot went into the ceiling.

Starting a new life

1 a) He was fed up with it.
   b) He had made one for his dog. His dog liked it and so did other dogs, so he decided to try making and selling them.
   c) He got bored with making dog beds. He got 'itchy feet'. He wanted to do something else.
   d) It was one of the things he did as a hobby. Not many other people had started a small brewery at that time. It was something different.
   e) No, he thinks it is a business you can build up and keep going for life.
   f) He doesn't like working with other people. He is afraid he would take things easy if he had someone else working for him.

Key

A weekend in London

	MORNING	AFTERNOON	EVENING
FRIDAY			6.30 Arrive at hotel. 7.30 Walk in West End. Free after walk.
SATURDAY	9.30 Walk through London Parks. 11.00 Changing of the Guard.	Visit Houses of Parliament; or shopping; or river trip to Greenwich. Meet 2.00 at Westminster Pier.	Theatre visit – musical or straight play.
SUNDAY	10.30 Visit to street market – Petticoat Lane. London pub for lunch.	Leave hotel. Return home.	

1 Two important pieces of advice:
    Wear comfortable shoes.
    Look after money very carefully.

Voices in my head

1 The main points of the story:
  a) He was affected in one ear. It did not make him completely deaf but he had difficulty hearing things.
  b) He had an abscess in his left ear. When it burst it left behind a tiny scab that restricted the normal movement of his eardrum.
  c) He was going to a special hospital in London.
  d) He saw another specialist; he got a second opinion.

Show jumping

Listening

1 a) Springtime – the first horse.
  b) Fence number nine (upright).
  c) It was cold and raining.
  d) First horse – Springtime – 8 faults.
    Second horse – Dartmoor – 12 faults.

Key

2 a) He's about 50, or possibly well over this age.
   b) No, it is his second horse.
   c) High jumps. (The Puissance is a special competition that ends with a very high wall to jump.)

After listening

1 Springtime hit fences 2 and 10.
   Dartmoor hit fences 9, 10 and 11.

2 Fence 1   Brick wall
         2/5   Rustic oxer
         3   Gate
         6   Planks
         8   Rustic triple bar
         9/12   Upright (post and rails)
         11   Water jump

Football

Listening

1 a) 2–2.
   b) Liverpool.
   c) After about eleven minutes of the second half.
   d) Brian Greenhof.
   e) Alan Hansen.
   f) In Manchester United's half.

After listening once

1 Alan Hansen – Liverpool   Brian Greenhof – Manchester United
   Gordon McQueen – Manchester United   Emlyn Hughes – Liverpool
   Gary Bailey – Manchester United   Steve Heighway – Liverpool
   Phil Neal – Liverpool   Arthur Albiston – Manchester United
   Ray Kennedy – Liverpool   Kenny Dalglish – Liverpool
   Steve Coppel – Manchester United   Terry McDermott – Liverpool
   Jimmy Greenhof – Manchester United

2 *First section*
   a) No, they've been in three and are hoping to get to their fourth.
   b) That's right.
   c) No, United beat Liverpool.
   d) That's right.

131

Key

  e) No, it was his brother *Brian*.
  f) No, they are not very experienced.
  g) The Liverpool side is very experienced indeed.
  h) That's right.

Second section
  a) No, the score was 2–1.
  b) No, Alan Hansen is a Scotsman.
  c) That's right.
  d) No, this was his first goal of the season.
  e) That's right.

Third section
  a) No, they played injury time.
  b) No, someone brought Hughes down, so Liverpool had a free kick.
  c) No, Liverpool are used to pressure.
  d) No, they have to play again because this match was drawn.

3 a) a long ball down field
  b) a goal kick
  c) gone out of play
  d) lays it square
  e) a loose ball
  f) a corner
  g) hits it home
  h) lobs it
  i) cuts it back

Horse race

1 The horses finished in the following order:
  1 Jellaby
  2 Rhyme Royal
  3 Sexton Blake
  4 Effulgence
  5 Swiss Maid
  6 Palimon
  7 Fluellin

David Attenborough

1 a) The change that is forced upon you by the fact that everything is changing all around you all the time; the change that you can bring about by your own efforts.

Key

- b) The South Seas (Fiji); South East Asia; the Galapagos Islands.
- c) When you are moving from one thing to another.
- d) The happiness begins to wear off.
- e) No, you are changed because the world changes around you.
- f) It was a new challenge; there was a lot of money to start a new network.
- g) People around you are changing; you are getting older; you meet different people; you have children and they change.
- h) To own their own house; to learn how to play the piano; to grow geraniums.

2 David Attenborough might say:
- a) I think that if you stay in one place and don't change, the happiness begins to wear off.
- b) I think you are happiest when you have just finished something and are going to start something else. Change brings happiness.
- c) I can understand that, but if someone presented you with a real challenge you would have to consider accepting it.
- d) But you have it within yourself to bring about change. You can set yourself targets.
- e) No, there are some changes you can't avoid. The world changes around you and you are changed with it.

Mrs Victor Bruce

1 a) She thought that women should look after the home and the children and that men should be concerned with things like voting.
- b) She laughed at them and decided she was not going to join them.
- c) She was 'highly insulted' if anyone called her a suffragette.
- d) Nobody interfered with them, although some people booed and a lot of people clapped.
- e) She liked competing against men in motor car races.

2 They wanted votes for women.
They were successful in the end.
Not all women approved of them.
A lot of people supported them.
They held marches.
They chained themselves to railings.

3 a) She had a governess (so was middle-/upper-class).
   She probably lived in London.
   Her closest friends were not suffragettes.
   She competed against men in car races. She once beat Frazer Nash, but never beat Henry Seagrave.

Key

b) She did not want to be a suffragette.
   She thought men should be in charge of things like politics.
   She thought women should look after the home and the children.
   She thinks women in Parliament have done some good things, although she was not in favour of women getting the vote.
   She was not interested in political questions.

Renee Wyndham

1 The three topics:
   Why she travels so much.
   The dangers you can meet travelling.
   The cost of travelling.

2 You can often live more cheaply in other countries than in England.
   You can stay with friends.
   Do not eat very much.
   Sleep in hostels.
   Sleep out.
   Walk a lot.
   Hitchhike.
   Earn some money. (She gives concerts.)

8 You are free from routines.
   You are free from the assumptions people make about you.
   You are free from inhibitions that stop you being the sort of person you would like to be.

Michael Parkinson

Listening

The five questions Michael Parkinson is asked:
How can you tell if someone is going to make a good interviewer?
When you have done an interview, how do you know if it has been a good one or not?
How do you bring out the best in people?
Do you stick to written questions or do you deviate?
Have you got a word of encouragement for young people setting out on a career as an interviewer?

Key

After listening

1. Q. 2 You have to 'watch it back' to tell. It depends on the director getting the right shot. The director can make it seem more interesting than it was.
   Q. 3 The main thing is research; knowing a lot about the person to be interviewed. You must know what you want to do. You cannot make it up as you go along.
   Q. 4 He does not have set questions but a list of areas to be covered. He does not often keep to these. You have to be ready to follow the conversation wherever it goes, but also try to direct it.
   Q. 5 It is a perfect job for people with talent, energy and ambition. You only need 5% talent and 95% energy. And there are no examinations to pass.

2. a) He suggests that a lot of people have failed. He says 'the graveyard of the BBC is littered with' the tombstones of people who have tried it and failed.
   b) The ability to get on with people.
   c) Robert Mitchum's longest reply was 'Yes'. Michael Parkinson had to use all his research and all the questions he had thought of to get through the interview.

The mind's eye

1. These are some of the things you could say:

   They've got every kind of book you would expect to find in a Public Library; all sorts of literature, travel books, history, thrillers, biography – and the Bible.

   They're recorded by professional readers. They take care to select the right reader for each different type of book.

   They also have a student library. Voluntary readers record students' technical books, so you could probably get the economics texts you are interested in.

   It's a very simple machine using special cassettes. There are only three controls to worry about.

   They have 1,600 volunteers who service the machines. When people write or telephone with a problem they notify the nearest volunteer to come and look at the machine.

2. There are two projections at the back of the platform. These locate the cassette. You only have to press it down and it will fall into place. At the front are the on/off knob, the tape start lever which you push away from you and the volume control knob. The cassette contains the spools, the tape and the special playback head. The tape is half an inch wide and has eighteen tracks. At the end of each track you turn the cassette over and move the playback head down to the next track with a button on the machine.

Key

May Day

1 Coronation Green
   In the streets of the town
   St Mary's Hall

2 This is one possible correct version of the information.

   Morris dancing is a traditional English form of dance and it existed all over the country until it almost died out in the nineteenth century. There is no long tradition of Morris dancing in Sussex. There they had a form of country dance called 'step dancing'. In Shoreham they perform Morris dances from the Cotswolds district. The dancers used to black their faces so that they could not be recognised. It is probably for this reason that they were called 'Moorish' dancers; a name that later became changed to 'Morris'. The bells are not used for country dancing, only for Morris dances. They were originally intended to frighten away evil spirits.

3 a) Shoreham is a small harbour town on the Sussex coast.
   b) The Chanctonbury Ring is a circle of trees planted on the South Downs to commemorate Queen Victoria.
   c) Dick Playall has been a Morris dancer for twenty years and is portly – a bit fat.
   d) The ceremony has been going on for twenty years without a break.
   e) They are thought to have both served the same purpose originally – to frighten away evil spirits.
   f) The instrument mostly used – and which you can hear on the recording – is the accordion.

Drakesbroughton Hall

1 a) Since March 1767. For about 220 years.
   b) Because it is haunted.
   c) The panelling in the Great Hall is nearly all gone and the staircase is rotting away, although the floor is sound. There is an air of evil about it.
   d) Cornelius Wilkes; probably one of the most evil and sadistic men who ever lived.
   e) When he was 25.
   f) In the dining room.
   g) It was very big and panelled. It was dark because the curtains were kept closed. There was an altar in the room used for Black Mass.
   h) They were idlers, drunkards and no-goods; rich and weak.
   i) His money, wine and lands had all gone – and many of his friends. He was 35 but he looked 50.
   j) His remaining five friends, and the servant.

Key

    k) Cornelius Wilkes threw an empty bottle at the altar. There was a crash of thunder and lightning flashed from the altar piercing him through the heart. A replica of the devil's trident was burnt on his face.
    l) They all died before they could escape – except for the servant.
    m) ?????????????????????

2 a) The house was built in 1587 and rebuilt in 1690. The family was still rich when Cornelius Wilkes inherited it.
    b) He inherited 400 acres of land, more than 2,000 bottles of wine, 20 servants, 5 carriages and a great deal of money – together with the house, of course.
    c) It is completely empty. There are not even any rats or birds.
    d) 20.
    e) 11th March 1767.
    f) Lancelot Sargent.
    g) He began to stammer and he mentioned the marks on his face.

The devil undone

Listening

1 a) He was sitting in a pub.
    b) There used to be a cobbler's shop.
    c) He was a farm worker before he became a cobbler.
    d) His wife's family was not rich.
    e) No, he only moved to the outskirts of the same village.
    f) Yes, he was 40.
    g) No, he got the gold immediately.
    h) Yes, he was 47.
    i) The devil flew through the window and was carried away on the back of a horse.
    j) It was originally called 'The Devil upon Dun'.

After listening

1 On the *same/very* spot where the *pub/inn* called 'The Devil Undone' now stands there used to be a *cobbler's* shop where a man called Zebediah Bayliss lived and worked with his *wife*. He was the son of a farm *labourer* and worked on a *farm* himself before he became a *cobbler*. He got *married* when he was 19 and his *wife* never stopped *complaining* about how *poor* they were. On his *fortieth* birthday Zebediah was at the *end* of his *tether*. Everything had gone *wrong* that day and his wife had not stopped *complaining* since *daybreak*. He badly needed money. 'I'd *sell* my soul for a *pot* of gold,' he cried. Suddenly he saw a *strange* figure standing in front of him. It was the *devil* himself. 'I'll give

Key

you your *pot* of gold, Zebediah,' he said, 'if in *seven* years' time you give me your *soul*.'

Zebediah was so desperate for money that he *agreed*. The *devil* disappeared and there on the floor was a great *bag* full of gold. The *cobbler* and his wife lived *comfortably* from that moment. Zebediah only *worked* when he felt like it and his wife had nothing to *complain* about.

Seven years later, however, the *devil* appeared again.
'Are you ready to keep your bargain?' the devil *asked* Zebediah.
'Yes, I'm ready,' Zebediah replied, 'but first I would like you to give me one more *wish*.'
'Very well,' *replied* the devil, 'but make it *simple*. We have a *long* way to go.' Zebediah made his wish. 'I wish you were back in *hell* never to return!' he cried.

With a crash the *devil* flew through the *window* onto the back of an old *horse* which *galloped* off at great speed.

The *devil* never *returned* and Zebediah and his wife lived *happily* for the rest of their lives.

When their *cottage* was pulled down, the *inn/pub* they built in its place was first called 'The Devil upon Dun', but this later became changed to 'The Devil Undone'.

Violence in sport

After listening

1 The table opposite shows what the people taking part in the discussion thought.

3 a) We need more responsible officials in football to stop the violence between players. Rugby referees are much tougher. They do not allow any argument against them on the field. They have much more control of the situation.
  b) It is a violent game but one in which there is rarely any violence among spectators. It is also an example of the difference between an amateur sport and a professional one like football.
  c) Rugby League is a professional game and it is also violent, but there is rarely any violence among spectators.

Key

Opinion	Did anyone agree? YES/NO	If anyone disagreed, write down what they said.
Sports competitions are good for international relations.	No	It seems that in football matches countries are taking war with them into the football ground.
Playing the game is more important than winning.	Yes	In a professional sport we're talking about winning, because that's where the money is.
Violence among spectators is caused by violence among players.	Yes	But a violent game like Rugby Union does not cause violence among spectators.
The fact that some sports stars are paid a lot of money is a reason for violence between players.	Yes	But it doesn't have that effect in Rugby League – a professional game.

Class in Britain and America

After listening

2 a) No. It is exactly the same as it was ten years ago.
    b) Yes.
    c) No. It's the other way round.
    d) No. The middle class is the most snobbish.
    e) Yes.
    f) Yes.
    g) Maybe, but it's a nice ideal to have, isn't it?

Key

Sex discrimination

After listening

1 This table shows what the people taking part in the discussion thought.

Opinion	Did anyone agree? YES/NO	If anyone disagreed, write down what they said.
Women find it harder to get jobs than men	Yes	
A law to make people give equal rights to women is a good thing.	Yes	Nobody disagrees directly but one of the speakers does not seem to think it is necessary.
Employers should be allowed to advertise jobs for men only.	No	Most of the speakers clearly disagree but they do not say so directly.
Changing the law can change people's ideas.	No	You can't change the way people think.
The person in charge of a meeting is called the chairman. If that person is a woman she should be called something else.	No	It's not particularly important. It just doesn't matter.

3 a) No, she says that sometimes you have got to stand up and do something.
  b) You can be sure it is legal if you put at the bottom, 'Applications from men and women will be considered'.
  c) One of the men did not seem to agree with the others that laws were necessary.
  d) A fairly commonly used attempt at a non-sexist name is 'chairperson'.

TO THE TEACHER

This is a collection of materials providing a wide range of realistic listening practice. The recordings in this collection cover most of the occasions on which the person receiving the language can be said to be primarily a *listener*. These are the occasions on which the speaker does not require a response in order to complete his or her task satisfactorily. Any response made by the listener need not be made in the presence of the speaker and need not be directed at him or her. Moreover, the response may or may not be a linguistic one. Such occasions form the section headings of this collection.
They are:
    Announcements
    News
    Talks
    Commentaries
    Interviews
    Telephone messages
    Documentaries
    Stories
    Discussions

Why no conversations? Conversations are activities that people participate in rather than just listen to. To practise taking part in conversations, the student should take part in conversations. Meanings are conveyed in conversations by very much more than the words alone. Gestures, facial expressions, body posture and movement, and the speakers' shared knowledge of each other are all channels of communication. Overheard conversations, i.e. those carried on by people one does not know, are notoriously difficult to follow and interpret.

Looking and listening There are many occasions when one person speaks and another listens, but where the ability of the listener to watch the speaker is essential for comprehension. Take for example the common

To the teacher

situation when one person explains to another how to use something (a machine or a tool perhaps). An important part of the listener's comprehension depends on being able to see the parts of the object being referred to ('Push this knob down like this'). Most of the listening occasions included in these materials might possibly occur with the speaker visible to the listener, but the physical presence of the speaker is not essential. This makes it reasonable to present the material on audio tape rather than on video.

Why listen? Like all other language skills listening is not something people do for its own sake. We use the skill in order to do something we consider necessary or worthwhile. Basically we listen for either *information* or *pleasure*. And having listened there is a result. We are changed in some way. We know something we did not know before. We can do something we could not do before. We have been reminded of something we had forgotten. We have experienced something new.

People usually have a *reason* for listening to something in the first place. The result of having listened is most likely to be related to this reason and is expressed in a variety of ways. A person might want to:

describe what he has heard;
explain what he has heard;
argue with what he has heard;
add to what he has heard.

He might do this in speech or writing. He might do it for himself or for others. His response might be non-linguistic. He might:

go somewhere;
make something;
draw something;
read something;
make no obvious response at all.

This set of materials attempts to reflect real listening behaviour. It does not attempt to teach the *elements* of listening skills. These are probably best acquired during the presentation and practice component of a good communicative, interactive language course.

Each recording is accompanied by a wordlist at the end of the section in order to assist comprehension at the vocabulary level. The activities set for the student are related in each case to a valid *reason for listening*. They represent plausible outcomes related to the act of listening with understanding. As such they are acceptable as realistic tests of comprehension.

To the teacher

How to use the material

In the instructions to the students the assumption has been made throughout that the class has been organised into small groups of three or four for work on the activities. The material may, however, be used equally well by students working on their own or by whole classes.

Ideally, each small group will be able to listen to the recordings on its own cassette player by means of headsets connected through a junction box. In this way each group will be able to exercise a degree of choice in the materials listened to. For in these circumstances there is no necessity for each group to work on the same recording at the same time.

There are obviously many learning centres where independent small group listening is not possible and each recording will have to be presented to the whole class through a classroom cassette player. In these cases it is still desirable for the class to work in small groups after listening together.

There is no need for the teacher to work through the material from beginning to end. If a class works on only one recording from each section the learners will experience a full course of listening practice. A variety of recordings is included in each section in order to provide an element of choice.

There is no single best method for using these materials but some advice can be given.

1 Always ensure that the *reason for listening* is fully considered before the recording is played.
2 In some cases the instructions specify that the recording should be played only once before attempting to do an activity. These instructions should be followed.
3 The learners should be encouraged to discuss what they are listening to.
4 The learners should be encouraged to co-operate when doing the activities.
5 The learners should be encouraged to ask the teacher whenever they come across something that they cannot work out for themselves.
6 The learners should be encouraged to achieve overall, general

To the teacher

comprehension. So a long time should *not* be spent on detailed questioning about vocabulary items and grammatical structures. There are no such sets of questions included in the materials. Learners should be encouraged to listen in order to understand enough to do the activities required. Comprehension of every word is seldom required for that.

7 This is a set of listening comprehension activities, not a stimulus book for discussion classes or written composition. Where it seems reasonable, groups of students are asked to discuss subjects related to the recordings and they are often asked to write things, but there are no separate 'follow-up activities' sections. If the teacher wishes to base a follow-up activity on one of the sections from this book, he or she can decide what sort of activity is suitable for any particular group of students.

One category of language for listening that is missing from this collection is drama. Copyright problems made it impossible to include interesting contemporary examples of this variety of language. Many recordings are, however, available commercially, particularly from BBC Publications. Recordings of popular BBC Radio and TV comedy programmes are already in common use in English language teaching centres and these, together with occasional extracts from recordings of plays can be used to complete the range of material needed for a full course of listening practice. The reasons for listening to drama will normally be for entertainment. The most typical result of having listened and understood is to be able to talk about the story, the jokes, the acting and the quality of the production.